ECHOES OF INNER VOICES

the past is present

"MANN TRACHT UND GOTT LACHT"
("MAN PLANS AND GOD LAUGHS")
YIDDISH PROVERB

STANLEY ROSNER

ISBN 10: 1492364223
ISBN 13: 9781492364221

Books by Stanley Rosner

The Creative Experience (with L.E. Abt)
The Creative Expression (with L.E. Abt)
Essays in Creativity (with L.E. Abt)
The Marriage Gap (with L. Hobe)
The Self-Sabotage Cycle (with P. Hermes)

DEDICATION

To my grandchildren and their inner voices:

Caitlin Shanna Fuchs-Rosner

Samuel Dylan Rosner

Sophia Raisa Corwin

Juliet Elana Corwin

Jacob Daniel Rosner

Eliana Gita Nora Rosner

TABLE OF CONTENTS

INTRODUCTION

YOUNG CHILDREN, LIKE young animals, are curious. They try to understand this world into which they were born. They experiment with the physical world to discover what happens when they throw a stone into the water, why leaves change colors and fall to the ground in the autumn, what is snow, what is thunder and lightning.

They want to know so they can understand and deal with the world around them, the world of things, of people, of other living creatures. This desire to understand is a natural and ongoing process.

But when the need to understand is transformed into a need to dominate, control, and manipulate others, problems ensue. We may experiment by manipulating and testing in the surrounding physical world, we may "train" our dogs, and we teach our children rules of behavior. But when the controlling, training and manipulating of others become an end unto itself, we are no longer acting in the service of understanding or satisfying creative curiosity. Instead, we are trying to prove our superiority in order to gratify our narcissistic demands for grandiosity.

The world into which we all are born imposes controls on us. We are limited by the characteristics of the place we inhabit including the weather, the geography, poverty or plenty, war or peace, parents or orphaned, etc. We are also controlled by constraints placed upon us as living human beings such as health, illness, height, strength, level of intelligence, educational opportunities. Our perceptual apparatus interacts with our environment as part of our genetic make-up. We interact with a world that, at times, seems to play tricks on us. Our perception of shapes and colors, even our own sense of equilibrium is at odds with our expectations and we feel controlled by such "illusions."

The Problem of Control

Man is obsessed with the need to be in control, to be in control of his own life and to be in control of the lives of others. He is fearful of not being in charge and of being controlled by greater and unknown forces. It's been said that man cannot conceive of his own mortality. The need to be in control is based upon the fear of dying, the ultimate loss of control. We counter this fear by attempting to live under the illusion that we are masters of our fate, that we are invincible and that we will go on living forever. This belief is a fiction and we know that it is fiction, but we act as if death is not inevitable. We act as if we will live forever and we attempt to prove it by climbing Mt. Everest, by tempting fate in myriad ways, by trying to prove that we can beat God, nature, and the odds.

We not only try to prove that we are masters of our own lives, but of the surrounding world as well. We try to prove we are not powerless. But we frequently have dreams of crashing, of brakes failing. We try to act as if we are in control when we doubt that we are. Many major discoveries are based upon this illusory quest to master the world. That's what Nobel Prizes are made of. This is not to detract from the many discoveries of Copernicus, Pasteur, Darwin, Freud and Einstein etc. Man wants to know and to understand, man needs to create and to experiment. But it is important to recognize motives and limitations. It is still to be proven that Einstein was correct when he said, "God does not play dice with the universe." We are trying to understand and to explain the inexplicable to the degree that we can, in view of the limitations of our capabilities and potentials. We create and we develop theories to explain the world as we conceive it and to explain the human condition. Ironically, the quest to grasp control of our place in the world ends up with our having to accept our own insignificance. The earth is not the center of the universe, man is derived from apes, and man is seriously ignorant of the motives underlying his behavior.

We have trouble living with ambiguity because we feel we have no structure or control over our lives or our surroundings. We seek clarity even when it is not present. We impose structure without enough information or data and we jump to premature and unwarranted conclusions (often with an air of certainty) because we cannot tolerate not knowing, not being sure, not being in control. This is the enigma of mortality. We are left with the dilemma of living while knowing we are going to die, but never knowing how or when or why. We try to figure things out, we try to solve problems, but for those who feel helpless and confused in a world of intolerable ambiguity, the desire is for resolution and control and, for some, the resolution is by resolving their intolerance of ambiguity by placing the inevitable in their own hands.

We fear our own desires and impulses to control our selves and to control others. We polarize and create opposites between our selves and others, between good and bad, between right and wrong, between the angel and the devil within all of us. To live in society, we are forced to suppress our wishes and fantasies, we develop inhibitory mechanisms in order to contain and control our more primitive impulses.

Society also provides acceptable forms of control when internal inhibitions are not sufficient. We define what behaviors are acceptable or unacceptable. Some individuals seek external controls over their impulses by gravitating towards regimented and structured activities. Becoming religious and following prescribed rituals provides security for many. Others seek out positions that are hierarchical and ritualized such as the military or law enforcement which have clearly defined rules and regulations. The frequency of socially unacceptable behavior with which some religious leaders as well as members of the military and police reach the newspapers and TV suggests that many of those who seek these occupations, do so to rein in their more primitive impulses and not always successfully.

Underlying tensions are experienced in the tug of war that exists in the conflict between man's quest for control over his inner urges, his instincts vs. the need to conform to the requirements of society. We live with echoes of voices from within demanding immediate gratification, satisfying greed and lust without concern for others or consequences. "Where the wild things are," is within all of us. How do we tame our instincts and what price are we willing to pay or capable of paying?

Man must find other mechanisms in order to live with others such as sublimating urges into art, music, science, athletics, etc. Animals also live in communities and develop cooperative colonies to work towards common goals. We also live under the illusion that if we repeat certain patterns of behavior, we can gain mastery, supremacy and control over impulses and desires. We compulsively repeat behaviors to prove to ourselves that we are in control and that we can succeed over past failures only to be defeated again and again. We stake our lives or our fortunes in taking risks only to lose (which we knew would happen from the beginning.) We try to turn the inorganic into the organic only to discover that the organic inevitably returns to the inorganic.

Persistent from infancy and for many, throughout life, is a fear of abandonment, banishment, and annihilation. Feelings of fragility and utter dependency are present leaving us feeling vulnerable. We try to please the powers that be, to placate and conform in order to gain love and acceptance and avoid rejection. In some instances, the price is very high with the "protective" authority constantly threatening, demanding more and more leaving the person with an uncertain sense of identity, a life of fear and an overriding need to please while repressing anger and rebellion. We remain a child while acting as if we were adult: we try to assert and to convince ourselves and others of our independence, while feeing dependent, needy, and hungry for acceptance within. We are kept in line and controlled by means of guilt and emotional blackmail ("After all I've done for you, you owe this to me.") Nothing binds one person to another like the glue of guilty obligation, which, in turn, deprives one of a sense of autonomy.

We all deal with the control issue in our own way. Some seek outside authoritarian control, some by exert strong controls over their desires and impulses, some by constricting and limiting their lives and others by expanding themselves living with illusory grandiose images. But there are many who suffer intense anxiety and fear, ostensibly over outside threats when it is actually their own feelings of fragility and vulnerability.

This is a book about control and freedom. Most of us thrive when we are given freedom to choose how we would like to live. It is difficult to experience freedom of choice when echoes of inner voices from the past dictate our choices. Many of us also find it difficult to accept limitations and constraints which are part of being human in the world. We not only try to change ourselves and others, but also to change the surroundings, the environment. The extent that we can do this is often different from our ability to do this without paying a severe price. There are limits on our human capacities to accept that things in the world are not always what they seem, that we can be deceived by our own capacities.

This is a book about conflicts that arise between our inner desires and the controls imposed upon us from the outside, often many years earlier. Our desires have their origins largely in our basic biological make-up, our instincts and impulses as well as urges to experience life on our own, to determine the course we want our lives to follow, to pursue our inner goals and to realize our potentials. Controls have their origin in authority, in parents, society, and our need to live together, the pressures to conform, to live in groups and in society. But the struggles for control affect not only the individual, but how we communicate to our children. Are they exposed to a peaceful home in which parents deal with situations in a caring and thoughtful manner or are our children exposed to parents who are anxious over anything new, different or unexpected. Such anxiety sets the stage for the way in which our children relate to themselves and others, by overreacting or underreacting, by blaming or defensively feeling blamed, etc.

The issues of control and domination not only apply to individuals and families, but to our relationship with the world around us. We attempt to apply what is observed on the personal plane to the larger field.

Our selves and our environment are part of a whole, a unit that is constantly changing. Echoes of voices from the past represent a background against which the individual as figure acts and reacts. Just as a circle of red is perceived as different in hue when placed against a background of blue or green or yellow, so our perceptions of ourselves and the world around us, are modified by our surroundings. Though our working title is Echoes of Voices from the Past, it should be clear that the voices does not refer only to echoes we hear that continue to influence our lives as adults, but actions, behavior, treatment we are exposed to from significant people in our lives. We refer to sounds, verbal and non-verbal signals and actions that impinge upon and influence us throughout our lives. We change our surroundings as we act and react to our dynamic world. The self and the environment are inseparable. The self as strong or weak, healthy or fragile interacts with an environment which may be harsh or supportive, caring or cold., representing the totality of the surrounding world – genetic and inherited background, Self - perceptions are changed as surroundings change and surroundings change as our percepts change. We may be controlled, but we also live or choose to live in a controlling world. The extent to which we have options to change the world we live in determines our views of our lives. Whether we have options to change ourselves depends upon the sense we have that we can or cannot change our worlds.

1

ECHOES OF INNER VOICES AND RELATIONSHIP TO AUTHORITY

THERE ARE TIMES when we are not clear whether a task is imposed upon us or whether we assume the task through our own choice. Man craves the freedom to choose activities, but he often disavows the choices he makes. "I did it for them" or "He wanted me to do it, so I did it." We often do things in order to please others, to fulfill their wishes and expectations. But at times, we are not honest with ourselves. It's easier to say "Yes" when we want to say "No." We disavow accountability for our choices. Though we willingly agree to do things, we are responding to voices from the past, voices that cajoled or manipulated or threatened, critical voices that have become internalized so that requests and suggestions are heard as demands and commands. " Please do the dishes" is heard as, "If I come home and you haven't done the dishes, watch out!" Are the ultimatum and the threat actual? Are they based upon heightened sensibilities?" Are they based upon other relationships that have nothing to do with this one? Some of us are unable to differentiate whether we are acting upon our own initiative or under pressures that are perceived as coming from others. Are we reacting to the context of the world in which we developed? Were we used to permissiveness or directedness? When the boss says, "I'd like that report tomorrow at

10:00 AM," we hear it as "You must have that report ready by 10:00 or you are fired." There is hypersensitivity to the expectations of those in authority.

On the other hand, many of us thrive on direction, on being told what to do. We are fearful of assuming full accountability for our choices and actions. It is frightening to make decisions and to be responsible for the outcomes. On the other hand, it is comforting and safe to be able to say that we were told or instructed to do the task. We use authority as a protector, an umbrella. After all, it is comforting to be able to blame someone else if something doesn't work out well. We crave autonomy, but we also fear autonomy because it is accompanied by consequences for which we must accept responsibility. It means making choices and accepting accountability for the results. We cannot blame others or take refuge in excuses. Most of us dislike being criticized, especially if we come from a critical world. However, creative ideas and initiative are inhibited, even destroyed by the expectation of criticism.

We strike bargains unconsciously as to whether it is worth expressing and implementing our beliefs and convictions or to keep our thoughts to ourselves and avoid culpability. Are we doing what we want to do, saying what we want to say or are we submitting to pressures by agreeing when we don't agree in order to avoid disagreements? Are we willing to assume responsibility for our decisions and actions or do we hold someone else responsible? Are we willing to take chances based upon our own judgments and to accept the consequences and learn from them? There are those who control through criticism. Is that the world we come from? Do we feel that we have the choice of conforming or not? If we are surrounded by a world in which our efforts are discouraged, then we often react with defensiveness, even to the point of relinquishing our efforts and our own judgments. By keeping us on the defensive, those around us bolster themselves by feeling superior and we feel at the mercy of outside forces.

It is important to recognize how the message is delivered and how it is interpreted, who is sending the message and who is receiving it. What is the figure and what is the ground. There are subjective definitions of authority that differ from person to person. Reactions to authority can take different forms with utterly different results. The person who cowers under the criticism of a partner, boss, spouse based upon underlying feelings of inferiority and self-doubt perpetuates and repeats a "dominant-submissive" relationship. Some seem to always be in the underdog position and they accept and contribute to such lop-sided relationships. We are unaware that we are contributing to such interaction. We accept without question that we are at fault and that we deserve the blame or the criticism. It seem as though that's the way things are and the way things have to be. We fail to recognize that we allow ourselves to be put in the doghouse and we fail to recognize that there are forces that put us in that doghouse. In fact, we unconsciously orchestrate the victimizations that we complain about. We will not object because we really believe that we deserve the degrading put-downs meted out to us. Often this is due to shame, guilt, or living with a history, a " ground" of criticism and bullying that are echoes of voices from the past.

Lew complains that his wife constantly criticizes him. It's as if nothing he does will ever please her. He's disgusted and has been fed up with this relationship for twenty- five years. He tries to please his wife, but she is never satisfied. This is the nature of their interaction. Lew knows that his wife will be critical. After all why should she change after all this time? But Lew keeps trying while knowing and expecting that his efforts to please her will be met with failure. But Lew gives his wife reasons to find fault with him. Lew is comfortable being defeated and his wife is comfortable being in the position of critic. This fits the inner voices of the past for both Lew and his wife. When Lew begins to assert himself and does not agree with his wife's badgering criticism, the marriage is placed at risk of dissolution. Lew's father and mother were clear in the way in which they ran the home. They said with pride, "We run a tight ship and it's our way or the highway!"

Who constitutes authority? This is highly subjective and varies from one person to another and from one situation to another. Is it a parent to a child? Is it a boss to a worker who cannot risk losing a job? Is it a clergyman who is perceived as God's messenger? Is authority viewed as benign and helpful, as cold and detached or as harsh and punitive? Is this authority someone to be feared or loved, respected or disdained? And who is receiving the voice of authority? Is it the adult or a defiant and rebellious child? What did the background consist of that prompts one person to react in one way while someone from a different background reacts differently? Do we come from a family which was supportive, loving and accepting of our mistakes and accidents or were we scolded and punished when anything went awry whether it was our fault or not. There are many families in which one child can seem to do no wrong and the other child is constantly criticized and found to be at fault. Though both children come from the same family, their experiences and their self-images are very different and such difference can explain the differing personalities and futures of the siblings.

From the time Jack was a toddler, through elementary, middle, and high school, he failed to finish tasks. Though he was very bright, he did not pay attention and did not do homework. He was written off as an underachiever with attention deficit disorder. As an adult, Jack was keenly aware of tasks that had to be done in his business. He was considered a leading authority in his line of work giving major presentations at national events. When he had an exhibition of his wares at shows, he was ready to pack and move the necessary equipment. But in his place of business, tasks could wait until tomorrow and tomorrow and tomorrow. He would delay sending out bills, responding to correspondence, returning phone calls. He experienced these activities as commands coming from external authorities rather than as tasks that required his attention. Teachers, bosses, even customers were perceived as authority figures who were telling him what to do, depriving him of a sense of autonomy and individuality. He could not advocate for himself, but he would not tolerate anyone advocating for him. Only if external demands and structures with defined deadlines were a factor, would he rise to the occasion. However, activities that were open-ended or ambiguous did not get done. He initiated activities based upon fear of criticism.

Jack was fighting against the parents of his childhood, now both deceased. His mother had been constantly busy at home and in her work.

Neither did his father have time for him. A nanny raised Jack. Parents were unavailable or bickering. They were always too busy for him and despite their lack of attention, they presented him with younger siblings leaving even less of their limited time and attention for Jack. Jack was angry and he felt confused and deprived. He was angry because no one really had time for him; he had no one who took the time to provide him with the basic sense of trust. His parents had little credibility. His emotional needs were not being met and he was confused because he had no direction and he did not know how to proceed. He had to grow himself. He was unable to distinguish between his desires and obligations, between what he wanted for himself and what he had to do in order to satisfy parents and teachers so they would not hound him. He became passive-aggressive and lost his sense of identity in the process. He withdrew and resolved to do as little as possible and only when that was absolutely required. Jack saw himself as a servant devoting his life to fulfilling the demands and expectations of others. He did not count. The result was that Jack did not know what he wanted or who he was.

Jack presents us with an example of the distinction between being "task-oriented" vs. being "self-oriented." When we undertake assignments, do we see them as tasks for which we accept responsibility? Are they tasks that we are curious about? Do we view them as challenges that we look forward to undertaking? Or do we view the task as a means of gaining favor with the boss so that we can get approval, special treatment, a raise or a promotion or even a way of avoiding criticism? If we view the task as a means of enhancing our standing with the boss in order to be in his/her good graces, a way of pleasing and fulfilling his/her expectations, then the job is permeated with personal overtones above and beyond a job that requires attention in its own right. The job is laden with critical and judgmental overtones that interfere with a focus on the job itself. Nothing interferes with creative activities like concern about being judged and criticized.

This personalized way of viewing the task at hand is very different from seeing it as a task to be done for its own sake, a task that carries with it a challenge that is interesting in its own right. Is the task the figure or the ground, am I the figure or am I the ground. To focus on the task requires a suspension of focus on the self and a shift to focus on the task itself. The task becomes a part of the surroundings that seems to call out for our intervention.

In the case of Jack, the judging and criticizing started early so that he had trouble functioning in nursery and elementary schools. His home was infused with judgments, especially of Jack as the first born and only child for his first years. Though he was labeled as having attention deficit disorder, his lack of focus was based on fear and shame. His sense of his own worth was related to doing his homework. It was not a matter of learning, but a matter of pleasing the critical parents.

Methods of dealing with authority:

<u>We can move towards authority</u> seeking to please, Often this results in identification with the authority. We hope to become like those in authority some day in some way. This authority figure is a person whom we venerate in ways that we believe would make us more desirable, stronger, smarter, and wiser, immune to criticism, etc. Under these conditions we are most likely to complete tasks on time and to fulfill the demands and expectations of the respected authority figure because we have a positive identification and we have internalized the authority. It is not that we are being forced to conform, but rather that we choose to. We experience it as a choice and not as coercion. We may also feel that we are beyond critical judgment so long as we follow in his footsteps. We meld with authority and we want it that way.

We feel safe and protected the more we can become the same as the authority figure. We attempt to do things, say things and act as if we are the idealized figure. We fuse our own sense of identity with the adored person in order to provide us with direction and a feeling of safety.

Under other circumstances, we move towards the authority out of fear. We feel that we must conform; we must obey the authority because of dire consequences if we fail. We act out of fear and not out of respect. We go through the motions of being "good," of fulfilling obligations, but with inner- protest which we must keep to ourselves.

Many people identify with the aggressor. They view the authority as the person in power and experience the belief that if they identify with the source of power, they will in turn become powerful themselves. Though they may not actually be in a position of power, they act officiously exuding an air of superiority and strength. They feel powerful, especially in the presence of those whom they perceive to be inferior. These are the people who always complain about the waiter in the restaurant, the clerical staff in the doctor's office or the taxi driver. Such individuals idealize those in authority and yearn to be in their position without doing the labor necessary to legitimately reach the position of authority. Instead, they try to act as if they are in such a position in dealing with co-workers who are peers or they assume a superior air in engaging in activities with others despite the fact that they are not better at the task. It's the tennis player who insists on giving advise to his partner or his opponent when his tennis game is not superior to theirs.

At the extreme is the Stockholm Syndrome in which the underlings, the captives identify with the hostage taker and identify with him as the source of power. It is not only to placate the authority, but it feeds the delusion that by placing him on a pedestal, the captive will become like the captor.

Both of these variations are seen in Ted. Ted is a 35-year-old married professional. He entered psychotherapy because of gnawing feelings that his wife did not view him as number one in her life and preferred her extended primary family to him. At every opportunity, she would visit members of her family despite Ted's protests. Their relationship reached a point where Ted insisted on moving to a different part of the country closer to his friends and removed from his wife's family.

Ted had intense needs to be heard and respected and he needed to know that his territory was separate and demarcated and belonged to him. He would tolerate no intrusions on what he considered to be his possession, i.e. his wife.

Ted recalled growing up on "the wrong side of the tracks" and feeling ashamed of that. His father was seen as lazy and lacking in ambition. Raising a family in the poor neighborhood, Ted's mother was discouraged and unhappy for herself and her children. She communicated these feelings to her children. Ted identified with his mother who insisted on raising her children according to strict rules. She ran a "tight" ship demanding that Ted achieve, conform and work towards goals in school and in sports. Ted did not want to be like his father. He admired his mother, her style and her aspirations for her children. Ted resented having to strive to be outstanding in his academic and extracurricular activities which he did to please his mother, but also to enable him to remove himself and his mother from the desperate straits in which they lived. He succeeded, but with the expenditure of much effort and energy and without mentoring and support from his father.

It was important to Ted to know that he was appreciated and admired for his accomplishments and to know that he would get emotional rewards for what he did. He needed affirmation of the fact that he succeeded against the odds, that he was able to shun the negative influences of peers in his neighborhood, that he was able to rise to a more accomplished and respected level. Basically, he felt that for all his hard work and sacrifice to succeed for himself and his mother, he was entitled to have his wishes gratified. In his marriage, Ted was now the authority and, like his mother in the past, who sought to live a life of respect and admiration despite significant forces against her, Ted demanded that his wife behave in ways that would enhance his status. Ted's mother tried to prove herself and her worth through Ted and Ted, in turn, sought to confirm his accomplishments through his wife.

Both Ted and his mother became militantly independent because the father was a failure in their eyes. They could not depend on him. They had to take matters into their own hands and to assert independence at the cost of a denial of dependency needs. Ted saw weakness and dependency in his wife's need for her family. He wanted her to depend only on him and to support and enhance his role as the protector in contrast to the way Ted saw his father. Ted need to be "not his father."

It is crucial to see Ted's behavior within the framework of his history and the background that virtually dictated his behavior.

Another form of moving towards authority based upon fear can be seen in the person who feels compelled to conform, and to have everything run smoothly. Unplanned or unexpected events cause panic. The underlying dynamic is that nothing can be left to chance because if anything were to go wrong, the feared authority would be disappointed, angry, and punitive towards the person in charge.

Meg needed order and as she got older, the need for order became greater. If something unplanned arose, even if it were happy and pleasant, Meg would get overwhelmed. She could not handle change in her routine and everything had to be planned well ahead of time. She could not deal with change even with her body. If she did not feel well, if she had an ache or pain, she would become very upset. She had to feel the same every day and, if she did not, she assumed that the worst was happening to her. She feared that she would not be able to deal with the unexpected, that something would surely go wrong and that she would be blamed for failing. Her panic, her rigid need for things to be as planned was based upon the fear of reprimand by the authority which she internalized.

Meg could not adjust to changes in her life or in her body in the process of aging. She was treated as a fragile child who had to follow a strict routine with no variations. She grew up with caretakers who were threatened and frightened of the world and foisted this on the child. She could not take any chances nor could she really trust anyone except her immediate family. This led to a rigid view of a changing world and Meg was stuck in a state of fear and dependency that interfered with her attempts to gain autonomy. Though her overt behavior seemed unusual, she was reluctant to try anything new or different.

We can move away from authority thereby seeking to place distance between ourselves and the person in authority. The authority figure may lack credibility or authenticity. The authority may have to be tolerated out of necessity, but there is an attitude of resignation that nothing will change. Rather, we muddle along attempting to bypass authority. Often the result is alienation, passive-aggressive reactions, saying "yes" when we mean "no," or devious manipulations. We try to avoid the authority, to avoid confrontations, we may do what is required and little more. We tolerate them because we must. We don't respect the boss or we avoid him/her. We may do our job and get it finished if only to get it over with and get the authorities off our back. We finish the task, but begrudgingly. We need the job so we need to appease the authority. We do what is required, but not happily.

Jeb finally quit his job after many years working for a boss who Jeb viewed as incompetent. Jeb tolerated his boss because he needed a job and he had good relations with co-workers. He tried to avoid contact with his boss as much as possible doing what he had to do to keep him at a distance and to avoid confrontation. The strange thing was that in all the time that Jeb worked at this firm, his efforts to maintain distance from a boss he did not respect, Jeb did not actively seek other employment. For all his complaining and disappointment with his boss, Jeb seemed to talk and fret about it, but did nothing. It seemed as though Jeb did not want it any other way. The fact is he was never close to friends or parents. Jeb was always distant. His parents were rigid and strict in the way they ran the home, everything having to be the way they wanted it. But periodically, the routine would fall apart, the house would get messy, the children were ignored. Jeb could not understand what was going on because there was no discussion or communication. The only clarification came when Jeb was 14 and he was told that his parents were getting a divorce. While this news explained the inconsistencies in the parents and in the home life, it was also the end of what Jeb perceived as something that was steady and constant. He was not that close to his parents and his concern was to take care of himself. This was reenacted on the job with his boss. As long as demands were not made of him, he was just as happy to do his job and to be left alone. Parents, bosses, authority figures had little credibility, but Jeb felt that was all he had. There were no other alternatives so he had to make the best of things with his parents and with his boss. So he went through the outward motions of doing what he had to do, but repressing feeling and emotions of fear of the unexpected. He was the automaton his parents wanted.

We can move against authority. This can take the form of open and direct expressions of resentment or passive-aggressive and devious methods to release anger. Direct expressions of resentment towards authority results in direct conflict culminating in angry confrontations with feelings of alienation and rejection.

More often we prolong and delay completing tasks, we are tardy. Despite warnings, we incessantly ask petty or irrelevant questions. We must do things so perfectly that we cannot get them done on time, but we certainly are trying!

Direct expression of anger against authority occurs when an individual feels forced to behave in ways that deprive her/him of choice. The prototype is the child who feels helpless when the authority imposes restrictions, demands and expectations that are not congruent with the child's sense of autonomy. "Do that now," "do as I tell you," "no, you cannot go out," "do it because I told you to do it." Such a parent reacts with righteous indignation and authority while the developing child experiences a need for recognition of her feelings and initiatives. Such treatment may result in the child or the adolescent rebelling directly. Parent – child conflict is permeated with yelling, arguing or even physical assault. Such open conflict which may start in the home, often carries over to relationships with teachers or bosses.

At the extreme are those individuals who assault others or who quit job after job after job in an outrage. But more usual are camouflaged expressions of anger in the form of passive-aggressive behaviors. The movement against authority is not direct, but passive.

Cathy was angry with her parents because she felt that they never had time for her, to listen to her concerns or to inconvenience themselves to help her. She also felt that her parents preferred her younger sister. Following her graduation from college, Cathy lived at home with her parents and just staid around the house. When asked to do things at home, she delayed or did things reluctantly and sloppily. When urged to get a job, she had many excuses. She claimed she was devoting all her time to searching for a position, but she never went on interviews. She insisted that there were no jobs available for someone with her qualifications. Cathy intruded her self and her opinions on every topic that came up between her parents though her opinions were not solicited. Cathy was angry with her parents. She demanded their attention even if the attention were negative. As dysfunctional as the home was, Cathy did not want to leave. She felt no urge to establish a sense of independence. Living at home provided Cathy with opportunities to disrupt the lives of her parents thus allowing her to express her anger at them. Leaving home would have relieved the parents of the punishment that Cathy felt they deserved because of their perceived neglect and mistreatment of her by them. She was giving her parents a taste of their own medicine. Her parents were fed up with her and she was fed up with them and they lived in a stalemate of rejection and revenge. Her parents represented authority and this same dynamic operated in her relationships with teachers and later, on with bosses when she finally got a job. Cathy was unaware of the context and the background that dictated her behavior which was destructive to herself and to those around her.

AUTHORITY, TRAUMA, REPETITION

Conflicted relationships with significant authority figures in the past and, especially in childhood, often lays the groundwork for the traumatized child to repeat the trauma with others in authority. Trauma at the hands of those who are responsible for the care of a child, leaves the child feeling helpless and exposed. The child's feelings of vulnerability make him a prime target for further trauma and abuse. In his efforts to try to master the traumatic experience(s), the child may unconsciously repeat the trauma with different individuals and in different ways. Though he is unaware of it, he is acting out a scenario that states "If I repeat this situation which terrified me before, maybe I can be in control of it this time." Of course, this effort at gaining control by repeating does not work and the traumatic experience is repeated.

Nat was an adolescent boy who was part of a group of adolescents who were experimenting with drugs. One of his teachers in high school tuned into Nat and procured drugs for him – at a price. The price was that Nat would engage in homosexual acts with the teacher. Though Nat was not homosexual, he rationalized his behavior on his need for drugs. His teacher was abusing him, taking advantage of him and creating intense inner conflict in Nat. Several years later, Nat became acutely aware of what had happened with this teacher and realized that when he was in the throes of his addiction, he was willing to do anything. But now, years later, he appreciated how he was damaged by this experience and set out to sue the teacher. His father was squarely behind Nat's efforts., not because of the teacher's abuse of Nat, but in order to get money. But the reality was that Nat's father was repeating what he had done to Nat and what the teacher had done. They both used Nat to get what they wanted. They did not really care about Nat.

Nat was vulnerable to his teacher's machinations because he had been exposed to his father's hurtful behavior towards him as a little child. His father mocked and degraded little Nat while simultaneously buying him things and doing small favors for him only to take them away or to demand things of Nat if he did not do what his father wanted. Nat needed his father and hated him at the same time. He could not trust him, but he was all he had. In high school, the deal that was struck with his exploitative teacher was not that different and in many ways repeated his relationship with his exploitative father. Now, as a young adult, his father wanted to use Nat again to sue the teacher in order to gain rewards which the father had every intention of using to further his own purposes. The cycle was on the verge of being repeated at Nat's expense.

Our experiences with authority figures when we are children and adolescents become a background for future relations with family, friends and even our vocational choice. Whether the authorities in one's growing up were reliable, empathic supportive or absent, inconsistent, unpredictable, and uncaring can set the stage for the child to react with fear, anxiety and passivity or with intense independence and drive to be a leader. A traumatic experience of note in this regard is the death of a parent at a crucial time in the development of one's life. It can determine whether one's attitudes will be punitive and judgmental or sympathetic and caring. It is not only the loss of the parent, but also the place that the parent had within the family, the relationship of the parent to the individual and the reactions of the family to the loss. This experience can be a life-changing and can change one's perception of himself and the world around him.

Marty's father died when he was ten. His father was a busy man, but made time to be with Marty and to attend his Little League games. Marty felt good about his father. When his father died suddenly and unexpectedly, the family fell apart. Marty's mother did not cope well before her husband died and she was utterly dependent upon him. Marty, at his young age, had to take over as much as he could and it placed him under strain, but imbued him with a sense of intense independence and intolerance of people who were needy in any way. Marty was forced to inhibit and deny his childhood needs so why shouldn't others? Marty grew up and became financially successful, but was intolerant of the emotional needs of those around him. To him the goal was to survive and prosper and to relate to others in terms of what they could do for him. He felt he had been cheated by the loss of his father, that life would have been much easier for him if his father had lived. Marty had to prove that he could make it on his own. Basically, he was bitter.

Death of a parent is a reality in some instances leaving families to cope the best they can. But it is not at all unusual to hear people who grew up in homes with both parents present to feel that they had to "grow themselves" because they could not count on parents to guide them through the everyday tasks of growing up from day to day and year to year.

The loss of a parent has implications for interpersonal relations, future vocational choice, political attitudes, etc. These experiences and voices from the past continue to echo in many ways depending on the particular individual, his experiences and environment.

2

ECHOES OF INNER VOICES OF THE PAST AND THE JOB

MOST OF US devote at least a third of our lives to work, to earning a living. Some of us have had opportunities to exercise choices and preferences. Many others do not have the freedom to choose and are forced to take jobs that are available and make the best of it. For the most part, work requires interaction with bosses, employers, colleagues and co-workers, clients or customers, etc. How we relate to others is as important as our competence on the job. Most difficulties on the job are rooted more in interpersonal issues than in the functioning in the work itself.

The problem is repetitive. For example, some employees get into power struggles for control believing that they could make better decisions or do the job better than the boss or other coworkers. Resentments and competitive struggles ensue which are echoes of distant voices of conflicted relationships with parents, siblings or teachers.

Whether aloud or mumbling to themselves, they resent not being recognized and credited for their abilities while others who are less competent are being favored by being reimbursed more or by holding higher positions. Such individuals feel deprived and neglected unfairly based upon past experiences, which haunt the present.

Basically, we tend to bring our families onto the job, into relations with bosses and colleagues. We bring our families to bear on our management styles. Family relationships and their unique characteristics become the ground with which we interact in our relationships with others, our working style, our ambitions, our collegial interactions.

For example, our relationships with parents often colors the way in which we manage on the job., whether we take charge, autocratic, laissez-faire or passive. Some so-called managers really fail to manage. They permit destructive things to take place without intervening. Those workers under their supervision become upset when unjust things happen to them and they are ignored. They may complain, but nothing is done to correct or even to clarify the difficulty. The manager often has his own problems. He doesn't believe he has the right or the knowledge to manage. He may have been thrust into a managerial position without training. Perhaps, in his primary family, he was managed as the youngest child with older siblings and resented being bossed around. Now he feels fearful of arousing resentment if he manages as he resented those who "managed" him. Managers and workers alike bring their backgrounds and family issues to the job. The individual, the manager and the nature of the job itself form a larger context of forces which interact with each other.

Cora did not respect her boss. He was well-meaning and industrious, but he seemed oblivious to other workers under his supervision who did not keep up with their work thereby placing additional burdens on conscientious employees like Cora. Cora was left to cover unfinished work that was assigned to her team. She tried to talk to those who devoted time to personal matters while neglecting job-related wok, only to be told that she was not the boss. Gradually, the entire team became demoralized by the lack of managerial leadership.

The manager can be overbearing and domineering. She makes demands shouting out orders without consideration of the workload that her employees are under. She may be insensitive and autocratic arousing the anger of others. But as manager, she does not care. Perhaps this manager was the oldest child in the family of origin with parents who left the care of younger siblings to her. She resented this role and became domineering and overbearing.

Some bosses lead in an autocratic style, some micromanage, and some are much less involved in day-to-day operations and are primarily focused on the bottom line. How we react to those we manage is a function of what is being triggered in us, whether we feel we are being treated fairly, with respect, or whether we feel we are being ignored and unappreciated. Similarly, relations with co-workers touch upon our feelings of being controlled or being in control, of being preferred or being cheated. It's a matter of action/reaction.

Zach started a small public relations business, which became very successful. At the beginning, Zach did much of the work himself, but as the business grew, he hired people. He was proud of what he had accomplished and he made a lot of money. But Zach had to be in control. Zach presented as a kind, caring and benign man, but he could not leave anything to chance. He would check up on his workers, giving them new tasks, making changes and generally managing them. Gradually, morale suffered and some complaints were registered via the office grapevine. Zach hired an outside consulting firm to evaluate his operation because he was beginning to lose employees and he sensed the discontentment in the business. Conclusion of the evaluation was that Zach failed to allow his employees to exercise their initiative and he was trying to manage everything too closely. When Zach learned of the findings, he became very defensive insisting that he just wanted to be sure that the business was well run. It was hard for him to trust others to do their jobs properly despite the fact that he screened them carefully before hiring them. He could not let go of the reins and delegate and trust the judgment of others. The business faltered, but a larger company bought it out. However, Zach did not learn his lesson and could not relinquish control. Zach, in fact, was very close to his mother who was very attached to him. She was overprotective and very intrusive in his life. On the surface, she meant well, but she was so anxious and so identified with Zach that she could not give him room to experiment, to make mistakes and to learn on his own. He carried this same micromanaging style with his workers.

Tensions inevitably arise in the work place. At times, some may feel overwhelmed with work because too much is being demanded. At times deadlines are established which are unrealistic placing too many pressures on individuals. At other times, the work itself is boring and lacking in gratification. Sometimes there is a poor fit between the job and the person's abilities or talents.

In all these situations, it is important for people to be able to express their feelings and to have a neutral, but sympathetic listener. We all need opportunities to express our feelings and frustrations without being judged. That is difficult to find in the work place. Most often, there is a job to be done and the primary goal of employment is to get the job done as efficiently as possible. Generally, complaints are not well received. Bosses become judgmental insisting that the task has to be done, that as boss, he is not there to hold anyone's hands. Complaints about other workers or about the job itself do not concern him as long as the job gets done. And often, in larger companies, complaints are referred to human resources. Too often this does not result in satisfactory resolution. People who complain are dismissed as "complainers," and women who may be openly vocal in expressing their feelings are written off as 'bitches." There is very little room to express dissatisfaction or complaints about working conditions or relations with others and frustrations build causing greater difficulties. Too often, complaints to human resources are thrown back into the lap of the complainer with the message that there will be no intervention or even no attempt to try to air the difficult and arrive at some resolution, a situation which, for many people is an echo of past histories of being ignored. This resonates, for many people, with family histories in which problems were dismissed and permitted to fester to the point of familial disruption. This is the background while the individual who is being ignored is the frustrated figure.

Erin was a responsible employee at a large company doing her upper mid-level job very well. She worked well with her subordinates

and with the administrators until a new manager came to her department. Erin did not have aspirations for this job since she had responsibilities at home that would not fit with her becoming a manager.
She was given an opportunity to apply for the position, but chose not
to. She was not resentful that the job was not given to her. However,
despite the fact that the new manager was younger and less creden-
tialed than Erin, she was officious and intrusive demanding absolute
subservience to her requests including irrelevant personal issues such
as dress and attendance at meetings that had no relevance to Erin's
responsibilities.

Erin was very upset. She also knew that her new manager had run
into similar difficulties on her previous job, which no one else knew
about on the current job. She chose not to divulge this, but did seek
some understanding from human resources also letting them know that
others who were being managed by this new person basically agreed
with her. Erin was angry. Human resources asked her what she wanted
to do about it. That was the beginning and end!

People on the job need to be heard. Some complaints may not be justified, but the person's feelings require recognition and understanding.
If there are employees who are chronic complainers, the reasons for the
complaining must be unearthed. They may be related to other aspects
of their lives in which case they may be referred to the employee assis-
tance program or to a psychotherapist. The issues cannot be dismissed
or ignored. Difficulties on the job, the absence of a sounding board, and
the absence of outlets for expressing feelings leave the individual in a
state of confusion and chaos. There is a sense of loss of control over one's
fate and one's judgment. Feelings of self-doubt are exacerbated when
there is no sympathetic (not necessarily agreeing) ear to air emotions.
Being left with feelings that one is being ignored or mistreated without
opportunity to discuss these feelings, only increases mistrust of the self
and of others. These are echoes of voices from the past. Parents with
no time or interest in hearing how children feel or to investigate things
that are bothering them. Parents who overburden an older child with
babysitting for younger siblings or who impose household burdens on

them leaving no room for them to feel and to express resentments and opposition.

The passive and unhelpful stance taken by the human relations department may have mirrored the position taken by uninterested and uninvolved parents. The leaves the adult employee who has legitimate complaints in the same position she was in as a child. There is nowhere to go, there are no avenues for expressing one's frustration at being dismissed.

Some people have talents and abilities that match the demands of given fields of work. There is congruence between their personalities and their occupational choice. Usually, we do well in occupations that fit our interests and our personalities. If we are lucky, we can identify those fields early, get the training and education needed to working that field and we usually are happy with our choice and god at what we do. We feel we have chosen wisely, we feel in control of ourselves and of others.

Many individuals cannot identify what they are fit for. Their goals and aspirations do not fit their talents and abilities. To enter the field of music when you do not have the talent is not going result in a happy match. To enter high finance when you really do not have an affinity for numbers and arithmetic is not likely to work well. For most of us, it is rather excruciating to work at tasks for which we feel unfitted, unprepared and for which there is no affinity.

Our society plays a role in this. We are closing schools that train people in the trades. We live under the expectation that everyone should go to college. There are people who are talented in the trades and enjoy being carpenters, electricians, or mechanics. Not everyone is high in verbal skills nor are they interested in verbal tasks. They work well with their hands and get pleasure from it. We need to help people find which fields they are good at, interested in and then to provide them with the facilities to train for those fields whether they are professions, trades or any other activities. There is no reason that one area of endeavor should be considered superior or inferior to others. Society's hierarchy based upon prestige and money largely drives this attitude. The more the field pays, the higher it is on the scale because we seem to believe that money provides control and status. This is erroneous since so many top earners today can be in trouble financially and/or ethically tomorrow. In addition, many children are not given the support and encouragement required to discover what types of work would best suit them. They are left on their own and told, "Whatever you want to do is OK. Just find something that will provide you with money and won't cost me any." And just as harmful is the attitude that children should be coerced into entering a given field without consideration of the child's interests or talents. It becomes more a matter of fulfilling parental expectations.

Occupational success often depends upon encouragement by parents. Olympians often attribute their determination and long grueling hours of practice to supportive parents. The same is true of successful people in many walks of life. People need to be heard, they need outlets for frustration and they need encouragement. The family plays an important role in choice of occupation and in success or failure.

3

Echoes of inner voices from the past; marriage and family

We bring baggage from the past to our marriages. As children we observe interactions between our parents. The manner in which father and mother, husband and wife relate to each other in subtle and in not so subtle ways, influences our ways of relating in our marriages. Are parents loving and caring or are they angry and bitter? Are they relatively consistent or is their behavior unpredictable? Are there influences outside the marriage that impact severely on the marriage and how do the partners react? Is alcohol or drugs a factor (as it is in many marriages?), Are job or child pressures or financial demands impacting? Are relationships outside the marriage interfering? Do spouses strike out at each other, do they yell at each other? Do they try to understand each other, to support each other or are they punitive and judgmental? Such interactions set the stage for the future marriages of children.

Does the child feel sorry for his mother whom he feels is being mistreated by his father, thereby laying the groundwork for the little boy to become the future husband who needs to cater, protect and nurture his narcissistic wife who takes advantage of him?

Does the little girl, who sees her father mistreat her mother become the woman who needs to marry a weak passive man whom she disdains, because he would not mistreat her as her father mistreated her mother? All the above forms a framework, an echo of marital relations that color the child's view of marriage. Parental interactions represent a background as framework for future marriages.

We bring our own foibles, sensitivities, and defenses to our marital relationships. Our underlying insecurities emerge in marriage and we become defensive or belligerent, we want to withdraw or confront. Some of us are fighters and others are peacemakers. The progression of marriages is not linear. All marriages go through up's and down's, through periods of relative calm and quiet and through periods of storm and stress. Marriages go through phases in the course of life when the nature of the relationship shifts and spouses grow further apart or closer together, when they become more volatile or mellower. This is a natural state, but it can wreak havoc for children who lose a sense of constancy and grounding when their parents have their downs.

The impact of having children on marriage is intense. Children can bring couples closer together, but they can also bring added stressors to relationships.

Essentially, we are talking about the Marriage Gap. The gap refers to the chasm, large or small, that exists between our unconscious needs and our conscious expectations, the discrepancy between what we think we need and want in marriage and what we really seek within ourselves. This chasm between what we think we want and what we can really accept or not accept results in mixed and contradictory communications. A young woman in love with a man who has very limited earning capacity insists to herself and to her parents that she loves him and is willing to forego creature comforts to be with him. However, she reacts quite differently when she discovers that she cannot do or get many of the things that she had been used to prior to marriage. The situation becomes exacerbated when the wife realizes that her husband not only has limited earning capacity, but is also uninterested in making a better life for himself and his family. He assumes an attitude that no one helped him so why should he help his kids? This places serious strains on the marriage. Why did she choose such a man? What did she mean when she said she loved him and would marry him under any circumstances? Was she living under the illusion that he would take care of her as her father did? Did she view her future husband as fulfilling her as her father did, despite the fact that he could barely earn a living? Did she dismiss her own feelings because of pressures to get out of the parental home or to make certain that she married before she got any older? All of these possibilities serve as a field of forces in which the individual's needs and pressures are influenced by the surroundings and vice versa.

A man who is attracted to a woman who is highly intelligent and ambitious claims he wants a partner who is able and willing to share responsibilities with him. He presents as an ambitious capable guy. However, as his wife's career zooms ahead and she becomes increasingly successful, her husband becomes increasingly passive and withdrawn allowing opportunities to pass him by. Wife becomes disenchanted with him and he withdraws further from his wife. Neither of them is able to accept what they said they wanted.

The marriage gap also refers to the schism that often exists between what the partners in the marriage communicate to themselves and to each other. There is a gap between unconscious and conscious needs within each individual and there is also a gap between the partners. She may say one thing and mean another, he may say one thing and mean another. It is not just miscommunication. It is confusion in communication, verbal and non-verbal. The gap refers to a chasm between what is thought to be acceptable and congruent and what is actually acceptable, between what one feels and what one thinks.

Harry tends to be introverted, withdrawn, quiet and self-effacing. He chooses Debbie, an attractive woman who is far more outgoing and social than he is. He wants her because he unconsciously expects and hopes that she will pull him out of his shell of confinement and loneliness. Debbie is drawn to Harry because he seems more conservative, stable and anchored down. She may be fearful that she could lose control over herself and she expects him to provide limits and stability. He counts on her to loosen him up. This arrangement can work well for many years. However, the relationship may run into difficulty if Debbie becomes frustrated because Harry is more conservative and fixed in his ways than she thought was the case. He, in turn, may be upset because Debbie continues to spend money they do not have and continues to be the social "life of the party," despite his protestations. In this case, expectations are not realized and the conditions of the unwritten contract are violated in the sense that the quid pro quo, the complimentary interaction that was expected, did not materialize. When the contract does not hold, power struggles often ensue. What starts as a cooperative venture becomes competitive? There is a replaying of echoes of past voices. Harry becomes more withdrawn and solitary while Debbie ventilates her anger by spending lots of money or neglecting responsibilities in the home. This kind of arrangement is often a repeat of what took place in the parental home in which one parent felt disappointed in the other parent. But often, marriages take place because one partner expects that the other partner will change in accord with his or her expectations, but not in accord with reality.

The difficulty here is a failure to assume accountability for the conditions of the contract. This failure to own up to one's expectations is understandable since the conditions and expectations of the contract are most often unconscious and not communicated one to the other or even to one's self. The only agreement is the feeling, the expectation that the partners will be able and will want to fulfill each other's needs. When these needs are congruent and when the partners are aware of what they are looking for and what they can expect, it is less likely that they will be faced with extreme surprises. Self-awareness and the ability to share needs, thoughts, feelings, and expectations, increases the likelihood that the contract will be sustained because there is continued communication of the ways in which each partner affects the other. Feelings are expressed, but defensiveness is identified and recognized as an interference with sharing feelings.

Mike and Jan had only been married for a couple of years, but the marriage had been quite rocky. They both cared a great deal for each other, but it seemed that Mike was insensitive to Jan's feelings. He would say things from time to time that would cause Jan to bristle, to withdraw from him. When he asked what was bothering her, she would tell him how his comments had hurt her. He apologized, but never really understood why she got so upset. It was only when Jan, herself became aware of the fact that Mike was critical of her and that she did not take his kind of criticism easily because the same thing happened to her sister in her primary family as she was growing up, that she was able to tell Mike about this. Jan was attracted to Mike because of many of his attributes, but his critical bite created anxiety in her and she withdrew. Sharing this with Mike, enabled him to be more sensitive to Jan and eased the relationship. At the same time, Jan was able to be less defensive once she realized that she was unconsciously over identified with her sister.

A common situation is the expectation that the future spouse will change or that "I will change him/her." Implicit in this is control and even domination of the partner such that they will bend to another style. There is a failure to accept the partner's values and standards as his/her own that demand consideration. The partner is not being accepted for who and what he/she is. Instead, there is a belief that he/she can be molded to fit the expectations and demands of the other. The expectation that "I will change him/her" is a major and common error in the decision to marry a given person. The implication is clearly one in which one partner believes that he/she is right and the other is wrong and, therefore, they are justified without question to pressure, control, cajole and harass the partner to change to their way of thinking. This most often is related to echoes of past voices that humored the individual while manipulating them to change their values, expectations and plans to coincide with the parental figure without consideration of the needs of the child/adult.

Mel was a down to earth guy who enjoyed watching ball games, fishing, and hiking in his spare time. He lived in a modest comfortable apartment He was a professional who had a job with the same company for ten years when he met Monica. Monica claimed to be in love with him and wanted to marry him. She saw him as a caring, considerate guy who would be good for her. Monica enjoyed going to Broadway musicals, she enjoyed dancing and she loved receiving glitzy presents. Mel was not into any of these things. Monica got tickets for the theatre, Mel went reluctantly, but told her he did not want to go anymore. He was not a "present" guy and he told Monica that this was not his style. Monica persisted in reminding Mel in advance of her birthday, Valentine's Day, and other times that she felt called for him to present her with a gift.

She was repeatedly disappointed, creating difficulties in the relationship. Mel told her again and again that he is not one who gives presents on these occasions. She could not accept this. Monica was out to remake Mel, but Mel did not want to be remade. Monica was upset because she could not remake Mel. Mel, in turn, felt that he was presenting himself honestly and did not want to be pressured into being who he is not. He did not pressure Monica to go fishing, to watch ball games or to enjoy the outdoors. He knew these were not of interest to her. Why should she pressure him?

Mel came from a family that struggled to make a living. Both parents worked and the children got jobs at young ages. They were not into frills or celebrations. Life was down to earth and aimed at bettering their lot in life. Mel succeeded in getting educated and in earning a decent living. He wanted to enjoy life, but he was not exposed or interested in gifts, shows, etc.

Monica, too, came from a family that struggled to survive, but her mother was very envious of others who had more and whose lives seemed to be easier and more luxurious. This is what Monica unconsciously aspired towards. Both Monica and Mel were responding to echoes from the past and though, in some ways, they seemed similar, parental responses were quite different and this was being played out in their conflicted interaction.

Once issues of control, power and competition become part of the marital relationship, trouble often ensues. This matter of control is seen in unilateral decision-making on the part of one spouse and in efforts to make the other person fit into one's preconceived and fixed images.

For example, Karen makes plans for repairs to be made to the home. She hires a contractor without discussing this with her husband, Jim,

Karen tells Jim the time, dates, and the expenses as a done deal. Jim is left with no options and he is rendered impotent,

Jim becomes furious and has a temper outburst. Karen knows that Jim is always passive, disinterested in maintaining the home. Jim has opted out and has told Karen that he does not want to be bothered with matters of repairs. He ostensibly leaves these matters up to her. When she assumes responsibility, he becomes angry. Jim sends Karen contradictory messages.

This unilateral decision-making is a form of passive- aggressive interaction resulting in serious damage to the relationship. But Jim has opted out and has invited Karen to take the initiative. It may manifest itself in outright arguing, in disagreements over money, in the form of withholding sex or in contradictory styles in child rearing. The difficulty is that both spouses fail to assume accountability for what took place. This too represents echoes of past voices which resound with beliefs based upon avoiding and evading accountability, finding excuses and defensively avoiding culpability for action

Other than the marital relationship, there are control issues between parents and children that will be discussed in the next chapter. However, there are parents who feel the need to control the lives of their adult children, often by interfering with their lives and their relationships. They also control the expectations of their adult children, largely through money and inheritance. In some cases, the control, in the guise of meaning well and having the best of intentions, is continued after the parent dies, a kind of control beyond the grave. In some instances, the adult child seeks to wrest control from the parents by living with expectations and even plans for their future life utilizing the inheritance money after the parent dies, an expectation based on a sense of entitlement and by "evening up the score."

The control of adult children is a potent factor not only in relationships between the married children, but between parents and their children and even grandchildren. Parents have trouble allowing their adult children to have autonomy and sometimes this is aided and abetted by the child who seeks the parents' advice or complains to the parents about the marriage, about children, about money, etc. thereby opening the door for the parents to inject their opinions. Growing up is growing away from, but many people have trouble letting go and taking on the responsibilities for their choices. Unconsciously they maintain attachments that provide security, but involves reliance on the parents, thereby giving them permission to intrude into the lives of adult children.

Nancy, a widowed woman in her sixties was constantly worried about her daughter who married a man who worked hard, but was not terribly ambitious about advancing himself in life. He was quite content doing his job and coming home to relax, though he did help around the house and had a good relationship with his children. He earned a living, but it was necessary for his wife, (Nancy's daughter) to work. However, his wife wanted to work. She was educated and had a career that she enjoyed. However, Nancy had not worked when she was married and raised her children and could not grasp why her daughter should want to or have to work. She would raise questions with her daughter as to why her son-in-law was not more ambitious, why he could not support the family without additional income. Such comments were divisive causing conflict between her daughter and son-in-law. Nancy also pressured her daughter to spend more time with her and to do more things with her. This was not possible with her daughter's responsibilities with her job, children and with her home, but Nancy would not let up on her daughter. In such an example, Nancy had to be in control even if it meant creating problems in her daughter's life. Her daughter was unable to confront her mother directly with her resentment at her divisive intrusions. Her unconscious needs were to maintain close ties to her mother even if this meant complaining about her marriage to her mother who would then feel justified in her intrusions.

4

ECHOES OF INNER VOICES OF THE PAST AND CHILD REARING

ORIGINS OF THE INNER VOICES

UNLIKE PREVIOUS GENERATIONS, there is now freedom to choose whether and when to have children. Some couples agree not to have children prior to the marriage. It is explicit and both partners agree. Sometimes they decide to have a child after several years of marriage and are able to do so later in life. At times, they decide to have a child only to discover that their biological clock has expired and they cannot.

Often, the decision not to have children is prompted by echoes of voices from the past, unhappy memories of childhood or beliefs that the world would be better off without increasing the population.

Such echoes are often reminders of how destructive and toxic one's parents were, how years of their lives were and perhaps, still are, filled with fears, self-doubts and anxieties. They may be concerned that they too will be toxic mothers or fathers and choose not to have children because they don't trust themselves to be able to do a better job in raising their children. They just don't want to take the chance. The choice is based upon the individual placed in the context of his or her background. What we refer to as "freedom of choice" is always a combination of the individual's conscious, unconscious, background, experiences, and the contemporary scene.

There are circumstances when there is no choice, when there are issues of infertility in either or both mates. Such situations often lead to turmoil and conflict with guilt and blame, with self and other recriminations. If the couple decides to proceed with infertility treatments, these often require scheduled timing of sexual relations, injections of hormones that wreak havoc causing mood swings and severe disruptions of the marital relationship.

There are other situations that complicate matters due to children such as out – of - wedlock pregnancies followed by marriage, the single mother and pregnancy through sperm donors, the use of surrogate mother or in vitro fertilization.

Other complications are found in children of divorce such as conflicts over custody, visitation, etc. Whatever the issues may be around pregnancy and child bearing, we are now more in control of decisions then ever before, decisions as to whether and when to have children, with whom and under what circumstances. Scientific, medical, biological factors are increasingly under our control. What are often not under control are unconscious factors that influence decisions to have or not to have children and the multitude of factors entering into child rearing.

These reality-based, biological, and historical and unconscious factors represent the background and the context within which decisions concerning the decision to have children is made.

What are children? Who are they and why do we want them?

How do we feel about the child within us? Has the voice of the child been silenced? Is it crying? Is it able to be expressed? Is the voice of the child heard? What happened to the zest, the vitality, and the energy that comes with being a child? Is the child's voice within us a voice to be squelched, inhibited, repressed or does it represent a force to be cherished and encouraged? Is the voice of the inner child a voice to be heard, recognized as an expression of creativity? Or is the child within us a wild animal that must be trained, controlled, regimented like a little tin soldier. Does he have a right to be free and happy, to be loved and, cared for and protected.

Does the inner child have a right to feel and express emotions. Many children are told: "Stop your crying, stop acting like a baby, stop nagging, big children don't act like that" etc. We fail to accept that children go through developmental phases and there is an unfolding process that takes place at different rates for different children. We, as parents, are so fearful that our children won't be "normal" or won't be "outstanding" that we become glued to charts that describe the pace of development, as if they were chiseled in stone. We (and some of our doctors and educators) don't allow for individual differences and for abilities to emerge with time. We become anxious if we are not right on the line on the chart called "normal." And our anxiety leads us to do dumb things. We rush, often with the advice of so-called experts, to have children evaluated, tutored, to undertake special training, etc. though many of these problems clear up with time. Generally, the anxiety and the special treatment "because you can't do this or that" is transmitted to the child causing problems of its own.

The answers to these questions determine parenting styles.

There are those who believe in a laissez-faire approach to child rearing. "Children will be fine if left alone. The parents' job is to nurture and care for the child, keep it out of harm's way and leave it alone. Nature will do the rest." However, children thrive on knowing that parents are interested and tuned into them, their friends, their experiences. Children do not want to be bombarded with questions, information or directions. But neither do they want to feel that no one cares.

Harry's mother and father were both college professors who were very involved in their teaching and research. They had Harry who was a cute, smart nine year old who did well in school, but seemed to be losing interest in some of the activities that had been involved in earlier. No one noticed this and life went on. Harry withdrew from more activities and was moping around the house more and more. Parents paid no attention. When Harry's marks in school began to drop, his parents were called into school. It was only when they had a meeting with the guidance counselor that they became aware that his marks and his school attendance were becoming a problem. This came as a shock and surprise to the parents. When they tried to talk to Harry, he snubbed them and told them to leave him alone. It was only when they faced the fact that something was wrong and told Harry of their concern that he broke down and told them how alone he felt and how resentful he was of his parents' preoccupations with their work. He told them how shut out and alone he felt except for the limited time when they went on vacation. Harry's parents began to spend more time with him and to involve themselves more in his activities and gradually things improved. His parent's distance and lack of interest in him caused Harry to withdraw from friends and activities. He did not feel free to express his feelings because his parents were so busy and so important. His parents thought Harry was fine and that he would find his way if they did not bother him. They were fearful of being too bossy. They went to the other extreme of ignoring Harry and failed to recognize that kids need to feel that their parents are present and involved, though not controlling.

There is the pedagogical approach in which children must be taught to grow up. They must be shown the way because they really don't know anything and we, their parents, must teach them everything. This is rationalized on the grounds that adults must educate their children. Of course, this is true, but frequently it represents a way of dominating children and controlling them. We know better and therefore, we are justified in explaining everything to the child. However, this process is also in the service of proving our superiority, our need to impress our children with how smart we are and to convince out children and ourselves how much we care. It is a means of bolstering our egos, too often at the expense of the child who wants a relationship rather than a lesson.

Sarai was a smart seven year old who asked her mother a question about all the birds she saw flying around in her neighborhood. The next thing she knew, her mother brought home five books on birds and insisted on reading them to Sarai. She also took her on several occasions to the bird sanctuary. Mother thought she was doing the right thing educating her daughter about birds. But by the time they finished two of the books, Sarai never talked or asked about birds again and she did not want to go to the bird sanctuary. What might have been a stimulating experience turned into a negative one because mother became overbearing in her need to be a teaching mother. But, alas, mother did not learn.

There is the <u>appendage</u> approach in which children are treated as if they are an extension of the parent and a reflection to the world of the quality of parenting that the child is receiving. The child is less important and primarily a vehicle for the parent to show off his capabilities. It's as if the role of the child is to make the parent proud and to earn her or him respect. The child is not accorded an identity of his own. His role in life is to show the world how great his parents are. As his parent and the one who bore and raised him, he owes it to me to demonstrate to others what a good job I've done.

Consider the following scenario

Max is my claim to fame; my creation and he must make me proud. As his parent, I really do not feel that I have much to offer myself, who I am, what I have accomplished. But Max is going to make that right and is going to justify my life through his behavior. Therefore, I devote my energies to advancing Max in his pursuits. I will help Max with his activities throwing myself into them and enlisting any other help I can muster. I will make contacts, serve as an agent for Max, get him into activities and take him places that I believe will advance his position. This becomes my raison d'etre and is basically the only thing I have to offer.

There is the <u>animal trainer</u> approach. Children are basically wild animals who are dangerous and they live in a dangerous world. The job of parents is to tame and train the wild animal child, to bring it into line, to teach it every step of the way. At the same time, it is up to the parents to alert the child to the dangers that lurk all around them. Children must be vigilant mistrustful. That is the responsibility of a good parent. Also, the world is filled with other wild animals and our tamed and trained child must be protected from the other wild animals and must be taught how to fight them and ward them off. It's akin to a dog trainer exhibiting his dog at a kennel show. And since the dog is seen as fragile and valuable, it must be protected against the dangers of the surrounding world.

Though they were not aware of it themselves, Angie's parents were afraid of the world around them. Her mother, in particular, was extremely alert to possible dangers around her and her family. She was sure that there were sources of contamination in the elevators in her home, in the trains, subways, and planes. The home had to be bolted and locked with security alarm systems armed. Despite living in a quiet and safe suburban neighborhood, there was always lurking danger from strangers, deliverymen, and other families and children. It was mother's job to protect Angie from these dangers. She could not play outside without an adult present. She could not have play dates with other children unless a parent was there. Other parents had to be checked out before they could be trusted to monitor Angie's activities. Angie did not have a baby sitter until she was five years old. Up to that time, mother would not leave her except with her mother. After the age of five and only at the insistence of her husband, she interviewed baby sitters and checked references thoroughly. As Angie grew up, she encountered many social difficulties. She was viewed as strange, as overly concerned about too many things, very cautious, and warning others of possible difficulties that would arise if they took any chances.

A review of the different approaches to childrearing is bound to bring the reader face-to-face with the fact that children are subject to the problems of their parents. Children act out the unresolved conflicts of their parents and parents unwittingly impose their unresolved problems onto their children. This is particularly seen in the interruptions and interferences that impede the progression that is necessary for children to successfully go through their developmental stages.

Which of these approaches and others as well as variations of the approaches described above represents portions of the environment in which we rear our children. Our own childhood experiences as we grew up become the framework in which our own children are reared. We may be carrying hurts and resentments about our own childhood environment and we may vow not to do this to our own children, but we often repeat the same forms of harmful behavior unless we become acutely aware of the damage done to us so that we have the freedom to choose not to repeat the same mistakes. This is seen in the extreme in the case of parents who abuse their children as they had been abused when they were children. We need some distance and objectivity to be able to be aware of our behavior. For example, instead of mealtime being a pleasant nurturing experience, feeding the child becomes a battle of wills. The mother, anxious to foster her view of herself as nurturing, feels she is a failure if her child fails to eat broccoli or drink milk. Eating becomes a contest of the child's needs and desires at odds with the mother's needs to feel that she is feeding her child or, more likely, that she is getting the child to do what she thinks is best. The unconscious forces here could be many such as, mother's own problems with taking and giving, mother's problems with eating, mother's ambivalent feelings for the child. In addition, anxiety over eating is often aided and abetted by pediatricians who create anxiety if the child's height and weight are not "on the line" of the developmental charts. Any of these issues and others could be foisted on the child. The result could be that the child develops conflict with mother and eventually an eating disorder.

This same type of misuse in the development of children is seen in the eating disordered parent who hovers over a child's food in the service of making sure the child is receiving the nourishment needed when actually it is an extension of the parent's eating disorder that is now being foisted on the child.

Helen was the mother of four year old girl who ate when she wanted to and who had her likes and dislikes in food like many children, who go through periods of "cafeteria feeding" when allowed to. The pediatrician told Helen that her daughter was slightly underweight according to charts of normal weight for children her age and Helen overreacted with intense and persistent anxiety causing her to mount a campaign to force her child to eat high - calorie foods. However, Helen repeatedly and constantly had to make sure that the child ate what was on her plate causing tension and anxiety during the eating experience because no child of hers would be off the chart!. Instead, it became a matter of Helen's hovering over her child during meal times, which became long, drawn out and filled with conflict. This became so constant and repetitious that the little girl no longer paid attention to her mother's obsession. However, the mother convinced herself that she was being a caring parent who was intent on raising her child to be healthy when, in fact, she was gratifying her preoccupation with nurturance and food.

In academic achievement, we find similarly, that children must be on the "norm line" and if there is any deviation short of the norm, the child must be bombarded with tutors, occupational and physical therapists, they must be tested to make certain that nothing is wrong intellectually and neuropsychologically. This preoccupation with adhering to the norm has become a lucrative industry costing parents thousands of dollars when, in fact, many of these deviations from the norm represent delays in maturation. Maturation does not adhere to firm graph lines on a chart.

Toilet training represents another instance in which parental problems can interfere with and create conflict in the child's development. Toilet training represents an opportunity for the child to develop a sense of autonomy, of taking a step towards independence and self-caring. Instead, toilet training can become a phase in which mother would not relinquish control allowing her child to accomplish a significant developmental goal successfully. She needed to assert her control and domination over the child by constantly reminding her to go to the bathroom, staying with her and insisting that she goes with threats of not going places or getting treats if she did not go. A power struggle ensues pitting child against mother during a developmental period when the child is developing a sense of autonomy and independence. Instead, it becomes a battle for control.

In such instances, the child grows with lifelong difficulties representing pathological echoes of voices not only from the child's past, but from the parents' past. The child is placed in the middle of a battlefield.

Development is also interrupted by unconscious reactions of mothers to their growing daughters and sons, as well as fathers to daughters and sons. Well-meaning mothers have difficulty allowing their young daughters to become cute and pretty without feeling threatened. Some mothers also become enamored of sons and become quite protective and seductive of their boys with efforts to overprotect them and hold onto them. Fathers can become threatened by their developing pretty adolescent daughters and withdraw from them. They shift from being loving fathers to their pre-adolescent daughters to being aloof and distant leaving the child feeling confused and even abandoned. Fathers may be competitive with their growing sons who are strong, young and vital and, perhaps, the apple of their mother's eyes.

Though we are unaware, we express our unconscious needs, wishes, fears and anxieties in the ways in which we raise our kids. We may be conforming and proper individuals in our behavior when we wish that we could be freer, less shackled and less conforming. We may be controlling and domineering when we want to believe that we are doing right by our children. When we teach our children that they should be "good" and conforming, we might also be communicating messages outside our awareness, such as "let yourself go, you don't have to do everything you are told, teachers don't know everything, you really don't have to listen to your mother (father), grandmother (grandfather.)" Children are extremely sensitive and they pick up cues and clues from their parents, they hear the messages hidden behind the words that are uttered. But when the children respond to the hidden messages, we chastise them. We say, "Obey the law" as we drive over the speed limit or try to beat out the red light. We become upset with our children when they cheat on exams, but they know that we take liberties with the truth in our relations with spouses and friends. When we, as parents, communicate, "Do as I say and not as I do," we are causing confusion in our kids. We, as parents, lose our credibility in the eyes of our children when we are hypocritical.

Is the need to have model children a façade? Are both parents on the same page and are they communicating a consistent picture? If we believe that our children must be proper, conforming, and polite, do both parents have the same expectation and do both of them live in this way themselves?

The child from the "proper" family who gets into trouble, who becomes defiant, who engages in anti-social behavior is expressing a message. The child may be announcing his belief that his parent(s) are hypocrites who, themselves, present a phony façade?

James was a man in his early 50's who was very concerned about his 19-year-old daughter who was away at school. James and his wife, Jean, were very proper people. He was a deacon in the church and Jean was active in civil affairs in their very proper neighborhood. But when they learned that their oldest and first born daughter, Betty, was living with a guy on the college campus, they became extremely upset to the point of wanting her to withdraw from the college and come home. They complained to the college administrators. The whole family was terribly distraught.

But James and Jean at home did not live the starched and straight-laced life. James was always trying to get a better deal on things that he bought and he haggled and chiseled to get better deals even at the expense of others. Jean was not the typical female member of the community. She was rather "artsy" and "craftsy" believing that anything hand made was superior to goods sold in the fine stores downtown where most of the women in town shopped. James and Jean took pride in the fact that they trained their kids to be frugal, to participate in cultivating a vegetable garden, in driving older model cars compared with the latest top of the line cars driven by their neighbors. Without being aware of it, they were encouraging their children to question the "proper" values and standards of their upper class community, while expecting them to conform to those standards. The children were confused about the inconsistencies. Betty's behavior at college represented her way of announcing that she wanted to be free in her way just as her parents were "free" in their way. Parents lived in ways that were contradictory, their combination of conforming to the mores of their community while simultaneously doing things their way according to their own styles. Betty was doing the same thing. She attended classes, received good grades, and lived with a guy at college as other students did while knowing that this was not what her parents would have approved of.

To the degree that we can acknowledge and own up to our inner strivings, urges and impulses, to that degree we will be able to treat our kids with respect and caring. We will not view children as adversaries when they express themselves.

It is far less important that we, as parents, be easy going or strict than it is that we be consistent and honest. Children need help in the process of growing up, they need mentoring, consistency and they need positive role models. They do not need to be held in a cage or on a harness, perhaps in the same way their parents were. We, as parents with our personal histories, beliefs, inhibitions and conflicts become the field, the ground into which we bring our child. Certainly, during the early years, our world is their world and children perceptions and distortions of the world around them is based upon us and our influences upon them.

A neglected, area of consideration in child rearing is that of sibling relations. While sibling rivalry is common, extreme cases of rivalry are often related to parental factors. Parents who resort to comparing children to each other or to other kids as in, "Why can't you be like—" foster hatred, jealousy and competitiveness. Such phrases become echoes of voices that replay in many different ways. The message is one of downplaying the child and pointing up his/her shortcomings. It is not a matter of loving children, but of wanting to fit them into a mold rather than accepting each child for himself/herself and accepting that children have a right to be different. Children have different strengths and weakness, attributes and deficits. Comparing one child to another is not accepting them for themselves and setting up conditions for rivalry. Parents can be divisive. They say they want peace among their children, but they communicate preferences for one child over the other while paying lip service to the belief that they "love all their children the same." A father who is interested in football has two sons, one of whom can quote statistics of football players and who watches games with his father while another son is not particularly interested in sports. Without expressing preference for one son over the other, the father is closer to the athletic son while the other son feels left out.

Similarly, if parents compete with each other or are in power struggles with each other, children are going to follow the same pattern. Not all families are rife with bickering in the children. In those families where the arguing is extreme, one has to look to the parental relations and the way in which parents communicate with each other and with their children.

Echoes of voices from the past: "big boys don't cry" "big girls don't whine." Inhibit spontaneous feelings. While children overreact and encounter difficulties tolerating frustration, they need an outlet for feelings. Some parents discourage spontaneous feelings of emotion – happy or sad. They prefer children who follow the straight and narrow and behave like adults. We set the stage for sibling relations, whether they are permeated with rivalries or with attitudes of support and consideration.

The setting in the family serves to clue children into different forms of behavior. The way in which parents treat an older sibling filters down and impacts the behavior of younger children in the family. The father who is strict, rigid or punitive with an older child affects a younger sibling's feelings, thoughts and actions. Observing a parent's harsh behavior towards a sibling signals the fear that -"there but for the grace of God go I." The feelings is that the observing sibling could be next in line to receive the anger of the parent so that one better conform and be a "good" child in order to avoid this kind of treatment.

On echoes of abandonment in child rearing

A major source of anxiety that persists throughout life rooted in child rearing is the fear of abandonment. Fear of abandonment is not usually identified, described or even experienced as such. Instead it represents an undercurrent that sends shock waves in the form of symptoms throughout life. In childhood, separation anxiety and school phobias represent threats of abandonment that are experienced as the equivalent of annihilation or death. In adulthood, fears of abandonment may be manifested in the form of clinging dependence or militant independence, emotional detachment, pessimism and moodiness, rage reactions, widespread phobic reactions to everything and anything. Self-doubts are rampant and there are usually pleasure-defects and social isolation. Despite efforts at overcoming their fears by going through the motions of acting the part of mature and self-sufficient adults, those who suffer from fears of abandonment experience significant periods of insecurity and uncertainty. They fear closeness, they have difficulty trusting and they try to keep their fears to themselves. However, if they suffer trauma and they enter psychotherapy, some of these damaged anxious people can develop a working relationship with a therapist who passes their multitude of tests, When this happens, when the "chemistry" is right between the patient and the therapist, transformative changes can take place over time.

A most extreme example is that of Jan. From the time she was a child, Jan's mother told her and her siblings, that if they misbehaved, she had a valise packed with some of her clothes by the door and that she would leave home. On occasion, mother picked up the bag and went out the door leaving crying, frightened children. Jan grew up maintaining a relationship of guilty obligation to her mother. She resented her mother who failed to be a constant source of support. On the contrary, mother was seen as a defective lifesaver. Jan needed her mother. She was all that Jan had growing up. But everything was conditional on not upsetting mother because the price would be that her mother would leave. Jan wanted to grow up and away from her mother, but she was filled with fear and anxiety. Jan's desire to be free of her mother, free of dependency on her was her way of trying to relieve her abandonment anxiety. However, she felt filled with guilt for wanting to abandon her mother as her mother had threatened to do to her. Jan's mother berated her for not going out, for failing to start a life of her own while she shackled her with guilt, uncertainty and fear.

And consider Larry who was married and had two children. He had a good position with a major corporation, but he was not happy. He was threatened by his wife's relationship with female friends. He was threatened when other men looked at her. He mistrusted colleagues on the job lest they try to get promoted over him and he had trouble with bosses over and over again feeling that they were criticizing his work and preparing to fire him. His anxieties had no basis in reality.

When Larry was a child, his father got a promotion on the condition that he would move to another country. His father took the opportunity and without any preparation, at the age of six, Larry was moved by his parents to a foreign country. He had to leave the neighborhood, the school and the friends he was used to and displaced to a strange house in a strange country where the language spoken was foreign. Nothing was explained to him. Eventually, Larry learned the language and adjusted to his new environment. At the age of fifteen, the family returned to the United States and they no sooner settled in a new state than Larry's parents took him to a private boarding school several hours away from the home and left him there explaining to him that that he should feel lucky and privileged at having the opportunity of attending such a school since this would enhance his chances of getting into a good college. Larry had no choice but to make the best of it, but he was faced with cumulative trauma of two major separations and upheavals in his life. He felt unwanted, like a piece of baggage, to be moved around. No wonder Larry was terrified at the very thought of losing his wife or job. His mistrust and suspiciousness were hyper vigilant reactions to trauma.

Growing up and living with fears of abandonment is experienced as an ever-present threat of rejection. The child who is heir to this kind of experience becomes an adult who is torn by feelings of anger with desires to abandon the rejecting parent, but with feelings of guilt and obligation. The parents send a clear message, usually non-verbal, but at times, verbal, that the child should not bother them. The child, in turn, wants to distance and detach from the rejecting parent, but is left with feelings of emptiness and nothingness. It means accepting the fact that the parent is out of their life forever, dead, but not dead. This is bitter, painful and filled with feelings of failure. He/she is conflicted. Reaching out means risking being rejected and dismissed. Dismissing the parents means living with feelings of self-doubt and torment?

Divorce is particularly traumatic to those whose past voices echo a history of abandonment, especially if the spouse initiates the divorce proceedings against the wishes of the person with abandonment issues. The difficulty lies in the fact that the person who suffered from abandonment fears may have unconsciously pushed the limits of the spouse actually provoking the divorce process. This is self-sabotage and represents an unconscious compulsion to repeat trauma from the past by causing it to happen in order to test the permanence of the relationship.

5

Symptoms, Diversions and Detours

Introduction:

"I have so much to do, but I can't get to it"

"I'll do it later"

"I just can't get started"

"I can't finish it"

"I go from one thing to another"

"I'm sorry I'm late, but I just had to..."

"It can wait until tomorrow"

"I know I should, but---"

"The situation I'm in is terrible, but I do nothing about it"

Good writers become blocked and can't write; rooms are partly painted, but never finished; plans are made, but never brought to fruition; ideas are discussed, but never tested.

These are the complaints, the frustrations, the feelings of self-dissatisfaction and helplessness experienced by the people who hear echoes of inner voices.

Not only are they frustrated with themselves, but they exasperate the people they live and work with. It appears as if they could do something about their behavior, as if they don't have to behave in this way. But despite the irritation to others because of their tardiness, procrastination and delays, their behavior continues and nothing changes. Their defensiveness and excuses only complicate matters making things worse.

Often such behavior is attributed to an inability to focus, or to attention deficit disorder, or to defective executive functioning, or to lack of motivation, However, we are concerned here with individuals who often have histories of high achievement and high motivation in other areas and at other times. Well educated and sophisticated people encounter periods in which they cannot get things together. They plan to finish, they set the wheels in motion to get things done, they do the preparation, but they just don't complete the job. Such self-defeating repetitive patterns of behavior are seen in marital choice, difficulties in the workplace, child rearing etc. In the present undertaking, we refer to more specific examples of repetitive patterns that are also self- sabotaging. Why do we avoid completing tasks, doing things on time when we know that:

Gaps demand to be closed, but some of us leave them open

Unfinished tasks demand to be completed, but some of us leave them incomplete

Stories seek a conclusion, but some of us don't end them

Musical progressions seek resolution, but some of us leave them unresolved

Handles demand to be turned, but some of us leave them unturned

There are environmental tensions that are part and parcel of being in our world. These desires for closure are tendencies that are "hard –wired," even constitutional and unlearned and part of the human condition. We feel tense and uneasy when tasks are left undone, when appointments are not kept, when musical progressions are not resolved. We can't relax leaving things in the middle, we don't forget about projects that are left unfinished. A work in progress calls for our attention. The field, the environment makes demands upon us.

There is a built-in process that places a premium on relieving tension, on getting things done, on finishing a task. There is a need to maintain homeostatic equilibrium by keeping things in order. In other words, the usual and expected response to tension is to find ways to release and relieve it. It is uncomfortable living with tasks hanging over our heads, with jobs left undone. We are not pleased leaving tasks in the middle. When there are outside deadlines, we feel pressure to meet them. When there are no deadlines, we still feel that we should, we ought to finish the unfinished work.

We feel inner tension when things are left open and not fully completed and often we rush to finish the job, to get it over with. Even if prematurely, the uncertainty of leaving tasks unfinished causes uneasiness. We feel an urge to force issues, bring them to a head, get them over with rather than live in a state of uncertainty, in a state of limbo. Often, if we can tolerate the openness and the uncertainty, resolution will take place, new ideas will emerge, and we will restructure our perception and see things in a different light. But if we cannot tolerate the ambiguity, then we rush to finish the job only to realize later that we sabotaged ourselves by doing so, that if we had waited and not rushed, things might have turned out better. There is a balance between leaving problems open- ended when they are not moving towards resolution vs. forcing closure. Passivity, waiting for magic or some outside unknown forces to take over and to resolve issues for us, often prolongs a kind of obsessive and circular thinking. On the other hand, compulsively forcing closure prematurely often leads to regrets. There has to be a balance.

But some of us leave things unfinished. We may think about finishing, we may be bothered, but we do not finish. There are people who can rest contented leaving things in the middle with unfulfilled expectations and missed appointments. In such examples, we see the individual opposing the surroundings, acting as if the demands of the environment are personalized and are dictating behavior to us. It is not a matter of inner drive or motivation. It is more a matter of responding to environmental requirements. Man's behavior is dictated not only by his inner drives and desires, but also by his environment. But to some people, these environmental demands such as keeping promises, appointments, deadlines do not mean very much. Plans do not have to be kept; appointments are easily canceled. What are the inner voices that interfere with finishing, closing, completing or bringing things to conclusion? What are the forces that favor maintaining tensions, frustrations, and ambiguities? How do we explain this disregard of tension, this failure to remove pressure? Is it a matter of being immune? Is it a matter of not caring? Is it a matter of defiance and rebellion? Is it a matter of avoiding accountability and responsibility? Is it non-conformity or is it passive-aggression? Is it narcissism that insulates us against our inner feelings? Is it a matter of being oblivious to one's surroundings, of ignoring one's perceptions and feelings?

At one extreme are those who are beset by compulsive checking behavior, by the need to be on time for appointments to the minute, by the need to be meticulous down to the finest details. At the other extreme are those who make commitments, promises, appointments, who undertake projects and fail to complete them.

Behavior is the result of our selves and our environment. The self and the surroundings are inseparable. How do we react to the demands made upon us? Gaps demand closure, but do we respond by closing the gap? Do we ignore these demands? Are we tuned in to our surroundings or do we defy the demands made upon us? Some of us can leave things unfinished while others feel pressure to finish the task. Some of us tolerate ambiguity while others need structure and clarity.

This interaction between the demands made upon us by the world around us, the physical world or the world of other people, on the one hand, and the idiosyncratic ways in which we respond to the surrounding world represents a field composed of our selves and our environment. Was our voice heard and did it reverberate or did we feel that we were in a sound proof room. Were our expressions received with understanding and compassion or were they unheard or mocked? Did we try to be heard or did we give up in anger or in despair? The answer to these questions has a great deal to do with the development of self - perception. If you felt important and valued enough to be listened to, to have interest shown in you, then it is likely you will see yourself as a significant person worth being cared about. On the other hand, if you are ignored if other things or people often take preference and you are treated as an afterthought, then this contributes to your feelings of insignificance and may be responsible for your seeking a sense of importance in other ways and in other places which may not be in your own best interest. This dynamic applies not only to childhood, but also to adult social interactions.

Our dynamic world is determined by the interface between echoes of past voices and the present, between what is said and what is heard, between the figure from the present and the ground from the past, between the transmission and the reception of messages.

We all develop defense mechanisms in order to protect our sense of self-esteem, our stability in a world that we perceive in our own idiosyncratic ways. To some of us, the world around us, including certain people or certain circumstances, is perceived as threatening or comforting. When we feel threatened, we try to protect ourselves by erecting defenses. These defenses can take many forms. For example, if a task is perceived as unpleasant or threatening or if we view it as an outside force being imposed on us, we may delay tackling the task because we don't really want to do it or because we fear that we might not be successful in executing it or because it would be tantamount to submitting. We may give up pursuing the task altogether, despite the fact that we may have promised that we would do it. We fear failure, we are reluctant to admit that we cannot or don't want to do a job. Instead of admitting that the task is threatening or unsatisfying or not of our choosing, we procrastinate or leave the job unfinished. There is a quality of rigidity that sets in so that even our perception may be distorted. If we allow ourselves to relax, we may see certain geometrical figures reverse so that cube that is directed to the right, reverses spontaneously to the left. However, if one is tense and anxious, such a reversal either does not occur or takes a longer time to occur. If we are under pressure, even natural occurrences that are part of the human condition part of our basic make-up do not occur or are delayed.

Voices from the past echo in the context of a background., Such voices may cause high anxiety and fears of many happenings in the environment. They cause distortions and overreactions. The voices may say: "be careful because the worst is likely to happen" creating conditions for expecting the worst. Such echoes may also be a function of the way those responsible for our upbringing dealt with day-to-day situations.

Under other circumstances, in our quest to please, appease, conform, and avoid conflict, we may agree to certain demands when we really do not want to. When this happens, we are left in a state of conflict, confusion and contradiction. We may end up making promises which we do not want to keep or we may act in ways which we later regret.

Many of us live with the belief that we ought to be, that we must be all things to all people at all times, that we must be universal geniuses, that we can do everything. Such beliefs backfire and we are faced with our limitations and with our inability to live up to our own expectations and to the expectations that we create in others. We are also faced with feelings of anger at being misused and taken advantage of, a condition that we created. It is difficult to face our fears, to admit our limitations and weakness and to live with them. If we fail to do this, we erect defenses and rationalizations, so that we then have to avoid, evade, procrastinate, obsess and ruminate, perfect to the finest detail, and feel compelled to cross all the t's and dot all the i's. All in the service of not wanting to face the fact that we advanced ourselves as grandiose and could not make good on it.

In all of the above and what follows, the crucial theme is the tension between fulfilling urges towards autonomy vs. the demands of the world we live in. Many of us who find ourselves in the dilemmas that follow are symbolic of the struggle of Sisyphus who kept pushing the boulder up a hill only to have it roll down.

Our defenses may be manifested in the following ways:
The Law of the Excluded Middle: black and white vs. shades of gray:
We derive a sense of security by knowing where we stand, but often this security is purchased at the price of oversimplifying by means of categorical thinking. Things are good or bad, right or wrong, people are viewed as independent or dependent, aggressive or passive, innocent

or guilty. It's comforting to put things in boxes and tie them with a bow. But there is little room for nuances or for understanding the bases of behavior if we dismiss the underpinnings of behavior. Overt behavior does not tell us much about underlying drives, motives and aspirations. Unless we are aware of or at least recognize that what we see is only the tip of the iceberg, we fail to comprehend possibilities other than the most obvious.

Consider the case of Gertrude who discovered that her husband had a brief flirtation with a woman he worked with. This came as a shock to her. Sam, her husband, regretfully admitted his part in this assuring Gertrude of his love for her. However, she was so hurt and vindictive, that she could only view Sam's behavior as bad, evil, and deceitful. Efforts to understand the reasons for Sam's wandering were dismissed as "making excuses." Sam had to remind Gertrude of her dismissive behavior, her coldness and disinterest in him since she lost her job during the past year. He tried to discuss his feelings of rejection with her, but she did not want to talk or hear about the part she may have played. She shut him out because of her own feelings of shame at losing her job. At first, she would not consider his feelings or the likelihood that her husband wandered when another woman showed interest in him which provided him with a feeling of acceptance when none was forthcoming at home. Gertrude was only interested in his betrayal of her. By the same token, Sam could have tried harder to get Gertrude to discuss his feelings, but he did not feel that she was open to his feelings. He also had a history of feeling unimportant and dismissed. Gertrude's defensive posture caused him to withdraw from expressing himself as it had in the past.

Gradually, Gertrude came to appreciate that her coldness towards Sam increased his vulnerability to find acceptance outside the marriage and that it was not a matter of labeling her husband as "bad," nor was it a matter of excusing his behavior. It entailed a willingness to appreciate the impact her behavior had upon her husband, leading to his subsequent behavior. She was ignoring him and another woman was available and ready to fill the void. It also required Gertrude to recognize the anger she harbored at her previous boss who laid her off after years of working for him. She withdrew into a depressed state because her environment betrayed her. She was left with feelings of unexpressed rage at the shabby treatment she received (echoes of voices from her past.) She was treating her husband in the same way that she felt she had been treated. She had been oblivious to her own dismissive behavior towards her husband and the impact this had on him. Awareness of these dynamics came only when Sam spoke of divorcing Gertrude. Both of them finally went for psychotherapy and only then did Gertrude face up to the underlying dynamics that were at work. Only then could Gertrude could allow herself to be more understanding.

Gertrude grew up in a black and white world and expected that her life should fit into an "acceptable" mode. Her husband's behavior could only be tolerated if she could accept shades of gray.

The compulsion to repeat was shown in this instance as a need to categorize people and situations as good or bad, right or wrong.

Human emotions are complex and we do not do justice to the human condition if we try to oversimplify feelings. It is crucial to learn to accept that much of life is to be seen in terms of gradations and shades of grey. Our relations are not built around either love or hate, but rather upon feelings of ambivalence towards others and towards the surrounding environment. Close relationships involve periods of love and periods of anger, periods of closeness and periods of distancing and periods of neutrality. Accepting these variations as part of being human makes life more tolerable. To accept a spouse or a growing child to be all-loving under all conditions is not facing the fact that unconditional love is largely reserved (if one is lucky) to a parent's love for an infant who is totally dependent. Many of us live with a dichotomous view that goes back to infancy. The dichotomy is between the good mother and the bad mother. Mother is good if she fulfills the baby's needs when the baby demands gratification. Mother is bad when the baby does not get his needs fulfilled. This process, for many, continues into adult life. Those who give us what we want are good and those who frustrate our wishes are bad. Of course, logically and rationally we know that this reasoning is false, but for many it is emotionally alive and well.

This Law of the Excluded Middle, black and white thinking represents a background of echoes of voices and attitudes from the past. It is difficult to change beliefs that provide simple answers to complex issues.

Related to black and white thinking is the tendency to generalize. A few instances of something happening leads to the belief that all things are like that at all times. Joan tried very hard to land a job in a very competitive field when she had little experience and a thin resume. She was hired by a small firm at a low salary. She took the job, but after a few months, she was asked to leave. Months went by before she looked for another job because she was certain that she was not good at what she did and would never find work. Instead of considering that she had to find ways to improve her resume, she jumped to the unwarranted and premature conclusion that she was not employable in her field.

Procrastination vs. the need to get the job done:

Don meant well. He really wanted to fulfill the requirements and expectations set by himself and others, but something always got in the way. He couldn't get to the project. Other things just had to be done first. His priorities were disordered so that less important jobs were done prior to more important ones. It was not an issue of competence. Don was perfectly capable of doing the job. The result was that deadlines came and went and the job was not done. Bosses gave him extensions and made exceptions for him, but Don always pushed past the deadline.

To Don, deadlines represented authority dictating conditions to him rather than realistic necessities. His perception that others were telling him what to do or how to do it, despite the fact that he agreed, threatened his fragile sense of autonomy and individuality. What was a requirement of the job was heard as a command. As benign as the job might be, as soon as Don felt his behavior was being orchestrated by anyone else, he automatically rebelled. Deadlines were perceived as impositions, which had to be defied, extended, or ignored, all of which placed Don in an antagonistic and adversarial relationship with others. He made up all kinds of excuses, but he was compelled to make his mark on the assignment. Don was not fully aware of the motives behind his intense needs to defend himself by resisting anything that he felt was a threat to his independent action and his autonomy. Don was caught in a cycle of power struggles. Relationships were determined by his ability to be in command and to be free of outside intrusions on his decisions. His behavior was haunted by echoes of voices from the past.

Don's compulsion was to prove his independence and his freedom even when it was unnecessary and not an issue. He had to articulate his own spheres of influence and to feel that he was not being overwhelmed by others.

Tolerance for ambiguity vs. the need for structure:

Allison needed things to be clear. She could not leave anything to chance nor could she be patient. The job had to be spelled out in great detail with everything itemized. Nothing was immune from her need to cover all possibilities. She could not risk omitting anything. Allison was preoccupied with making certain that she covered all the bases. As a result, none of Allison's undertakings was ever finished since there were always other issues that might come up. Things had to be left open to other possibilities and other conditions.

In contrast, Dave attacked assignments with gusto. His challenge was to meet self-imposed deadlines and to finish the job and to close it out. Dave disliked uncompleted tasks, he disliked "works in progress." Too often jobs were declared finished when they weren't, when other possibilities had not been considered. Improvements could have been made if things had not been so rushed.

Allison repetitively could not be satisfied that her jobs were finished. She could not risk leaving anything to chance or to other possibilities. She had to keep things open. Dave had to finish the job, get it out of the way, and get onto the next task only to discover that in his rush for closure, the job was not really finished after all.

<u>Paralytic perfectionism vs. accepting that many things can be good enough:</u>

Betty wanted to write an article but before she could begin to write, everything had to be perfect. Extensive preparation was essential She needed a dozen sharpened pencils or she had to buy the best computer or she had to read more or she had to meet with more people. The result was that the task never got done because Betty was so busy preparing to get to work, that she never felt ready. She would discuss at length the project she planned and it was clear that she had good ideas and had given the project a lot of thought. But it was all in her head and never was put in tangible form, in print or on tape.

Betty had to produce products that were beyond criticism. In fact, her work had to be perfect. When she wrote, almost every word was erased and rewritten and nothing was ever finished to her satisfaction. She was threatened by the possibility that her work might be criticized or that suggestions might be made to improve what she produced. Her need was to produce work that was perfect. Since she could never be sure whether or not criticism might be forthcoming, it was better to never finish it. What manifested itself as "failure to complete," was essentially "failure to risk criticism."

Despite her superior intelligence and her many talents, Betty lived in fear that she might be criticized, that she might not be as perfect as she expected of herself. Her successes were met with fears that her next project might not be so successful. Success to Betty did not breed more success. Instead, success bred fear that she would be unable to live up to her previous performance. It was preferable to avoid the next challenge. Betty was dominated by echoes of voices from the past that shouted, "only A+'s are acceptable."

<u>Obsessive rumination vs. allowing time and room:</u>

Erica knew she had a problem. She had to think about everything. What if this were the case and what if that were the case? Supposing this happened or that happened? Erica had to talk to others about anything that bothered her. Everyone knew about her dilemma and everyone was ready to give her advice. She could not let the problem go and could not relax as long as she had to resolve the problem. But Erica was not sure whether she should try to resolve it in this or that way and until she did, she could not relax.

Erica was very dependent on others. She was filled with self-doubts and was unable to trust her own judgment, her own thinking. She doubted she could solve problems and abdicated her thinking to others who were viewed as smarter than she was. Instead of evading and avoiding making decisions for fear of criticism, as was the case for Betty, Erica relinquished her own judgment and her own thinking by seeking the answers from others.

Erica could not tolerate uncertainty. She could not allow time for thoughts to gel in order to organize and execute her own judgment. The stress of indecision was too intense and the solution had to come now. The resolution was to seek the opinions of others rather than to trust her judgment.

<u>Fears of failing, fears of succeeding vs. my best is OK:</u>

I can't finish the job, It has to remain a work in progress, a thorn in my side, an unfinished job that hangs over me and allows me no respite. I need to pay a price beforehand; I feel I never deserve to succeed because I haven't suffered enough. I can't finish because if I do, I might succeed and I don't deserve to succeed. I must persist in punishing myself by keeping myself under pressure and tension, always feeling I've got more to do. My best is never good enough.

This is seen in the young writer whose novel is never submitted for consideration by agents or publishers. The work is never finished, it always needs revision, It is never OK.

The doctoral student who has been on campus for 12 years, has completed everything but the dissertation, is another example. The topic of research had been approved years ago, the methodology had been approved, but it was never put together, never finished and the years go by.

<u>Fears of competition vs. you can't win them all:</u>

The problem is the belief that winning is purchased at the price of vanquishing the other person. Success is viewed as beating an opponent, with attendant guilt. There is also the fear that the defeated opponent will seek and gain revenge. Success is equated with Schadenfreude, the experience of joy at having vanquished one's opponent. Can there be victory and success without this being experienced as pleasure at the other's defeat?

Buck worked hard to complete his proposals so that they could be presented in order to compete for awards. Despite the hours of work and effort that he devoted to his work and despite the fact that he consciously wanted to win, he could never feel satisfied with the results. Buck feared succeeding even though he wanted desperately to succeed. However, he lived in fear that his competitors would be angry with him if he won. He feared that his opponents would feel that he would be pleased at their loss. In fact, he secretly feared that he would be thrilled at winning and he equated this with an image of himself that he disliked, that of Schadenfreude.

The background consisted of Buck's mother who was Mrs. Polyanna. She viewed her abusive husband as just fine. She supported him to her children and made excuses for his behavior. She excused Buck's older brother who bullied Buck mercilessly. She tried to calm Buck when he was upset with the mistreatment he received. There was no room for anger and hostility. Everything had to be smoothed over. Buck wanted to play football in High School and mother feared he would get hurt. He was discouraged from competing because others wouldn't like him if he won. He was encouraged to conform to routine jobs, never to rock the boat and never to try things that were new or different because he would stand out and others wouldn't like that.

The worst case scenario as a means of control:

Control may be expressed by taking over, orchestrating activities, in order to initiate change. But control can also be asserted in the form of taking the initiative and preempting the decisions of others in order to avert expected rejection thereby wresting control away from others, albeit at one's own expense. For example Sarah was not confident in her new job. Though she was capable and experienced, she had been out of a job for some time and was no longer sure of herself. She was convinced that her job was in jeopardy, that she was being carefully and that she would be fired despite the fact that no one said anything negative about her work. However, in order to allay her anxieties about being at the mercy of her boss's whim by being suddenly fired, she seriously considered quitting the job before she was dismissed. Sarah had to preempt her boss so that before the boss would tell her to leave, she would quit. However, the boss had no intention of telling her to leave and she was shocked when after tending her resignation, her boss asked her why she wanted to leave and announced that he really wanted her to stay.

Another form of using defeat in the service of maintaining control is seen when a smaller dog rolls over and exposes his jugular vein to the much larger and more aggressive dog who then walks away. Appease the more powerful adversary by playing weak, but wresting control through weakness. Many people find pleasure and satisfaction in enacting the role of the weak one in order to undermine the strong one. This is seen in the scenario in which one person abdicates responsibility for decision-making ostensibly leaving things up to the other person. When the other person makes a decision, the decision is then subject to questioning, doubting and undermining. This is a variation on the dynamic of victim – victimizer. When it is convenient, it may be easier to play the misused victim, but when it suits the situation, the victim then becomes the victimizer, holding the other person accountable for making decisions that are seen as wrong. It's a "no-win" situation built upon a background of manipulation in which one presents ones self as the victim or the angry domineering justified victimizer depending on what suits the situation.

The goal of the individual who has a borderline personality is to cover over and prevent exposure of vulnerabilities and the best way to do that is to maintain a superior and dominant position, indeed, to portray an image of invulnerability. Others must be kept on the defensive and in the inferior position. This is accomplished by reacting with intense rage when there is any threat to one's superior position. The other person must be subordinate and kept that way by unleashing rageful temper tantrums in order to maintain the balance of power and to maintain a super ordinate-subordinate relationship.

<u>Problems with the dependence – independence dichotomy</u>:

There are many conundrums in many people that revolve around issues of dependency and independency. There are gains that are derived from being dependent, but they are accompanied by other problems. It is difficult to accept the fact that it is part of the human condition that we are all dependent and independent at different times, under different circumstances and with different people. Let's consider some examples:

<u>The Peter Pan Syndrome – I won't grow up</u>:

What presents as a fear of being controlled is really a form of being in control, but in a self-destructive fashion. The individual who feels dominated as a young child is unable to live up to the expectations and demands of parents. The sense of failure is so overwhelming that she eventually stops trying to please, feeling that failure would be inevitable. The parent may be overly demanding or a sibling may be such a high achiever and a winner of accolades that she would sooner give up trying by taking refuge and comfort in not growing up, not learning, remaining naïve and unknowing. This may manifest itself in the form of not socializing, not being able to interact with peers in an age-appropriate fashion, in learning difficulties, in balking at trying anything new or different. She is not stupid, but she excuses her inability to learn or to succeed as due to stupidity. Stupidity is bad enough, but failure is more painful. To believe and to act as if learning and knowing is beyond her is preferable to trying and failing. She is labeled "learning disabled" early in her schooling and she is singled out for special treatment, but the tutoring fails to note that the problem lies in the secondary gains and gratifications of <u>not</u> learning. The tutoring goes nowhere. Jackie would rather live in a world of not trying and not succeeding, because succeeding might result in recognizing that she is not stupid, not learning-disabled, in which case, more is expected of her. She can no longer take refuge in disability and then success breeds more work and who wants more work?

Others in a similar position will relate to others on the basis of weakness. The message is that I am too weak, too fragile, so don't expect me to live up to your demands. Such individuals want to be protected from confrontation and they don't want to be held accountable. The excuse is not stupidity. It is, fragility or physical complaints.

Assuming the responsibilities of adulthood can be a pain. Who wouldn't like being relieved of doing housework, paying bills, dealing with the many problems of everyday life? But these tasks are part of life and have to be done. Unless one can employ housekeepers, secretaries, chauffeurs, etc., most of us have to assume some of these responsibilities. But the well-educated man would rather be supported by his parents or wife while he stays home and relaxes because he can't find a job (which he does not look for!) or the woman with an MBA who holds a responsible position in finance is constantly overdrawing her account at the bank because she "can't" balance the checkbook.

These dilemmas represent unconsciously motivated behavior. Despite the denials and rationalizations, this behavior cannot be dismissed as "habitual," or "accidental." The behavior recurs in the same people and is motivated. The motivating factors may be outside awareness, but the resultant behavior represents echoes of other voices that in time have become inner voices, voices that are a form of empty pride. "Before you take advantage of me or hurt me, I'll act as if I made it happen." Or "Don't expect that of me, because I can't do it."

The basis of this behavior is often the parental setting in which "father knows best" or "mother knows best." Efforts on the part of children to explore, to try things out are discouraged because the parent could do it differently and better or because the child will mess things up. Discouragement and self-doubts become part of the parent-child dialogue. The parent needs to assert the superior position placing the child at a disadvantage all in the service of bolstering the parent's ego.

Identity: dependence/independence: me/not me

It is hard to acknowledge and to feel responsible when there is fog surrounding our sense of identity. When we perceive ourselves in distorted and/or fuzzy terms, we feel vulnerable and we are prone to be easily influenced by circumstances and by others. Many of us define ourselves in the image of mother or father or hero. We do not have our own sense of who we are and who we want to be. Others define themselves in terms of who they do NOT want to be. The absent parent, the abusive parent may produce children who define themselves early in life in terms of being "NOT my mother, NOT my father." Defining one's self as wanting to be NOT like someone is negative and does not contribute to a positive self- percept. Instead this leads to a self-image that is based upon bitterness requiring a constant expenditure of effort to prove that one is different from, better than the negated parent. It is not simply a moving away from or moving in a different direction. It is defiance and rebellion based upon hurt and anger. Superficially, it may appear as if the individual is independent and emancipated when actually it is a form of bitter militant independence that is founded upon a wish to be left alone.

It is a revolution, a rebellion. True independence is based upon a gradual evolution of separation and growing up with an acceptance of the natural need to be independent at times and to be dependent at times, an acceptance of the fact that none of us is an island unto ourselves. As I say to my patients, "even the Lone Ranger needed Tonto."

Other voices, Inner voices:

The past lies in the present: the present lies in the past. Most often, leaving things undone, chronic tardiness, procrastination, and relating on the basis of weakness are long-standing motivated behaviors that stand out as the figure that is built upon a background of echoes of voices and experiences from the past. As noted previously, they are defenses we erect in order to deal with feelings of threat. We feel overwhelmed. Urges that prompt most of us to complete unfinished business, to keep appointments, to fulfill expectations and to bring events to resolution seem to be lacking and have been lacking for many years in many of us. What factors motivate us to leave things unfinished?

Undertaking an assignment is complex. Where is the assignment originating? Is it self-imposed? Can we own the fact that it is our choice or do we experience the task as being imposed upon us by someone else?

If a job is assigned, what are the conditions? Do we want to do it? Do we hate doing it? Do we resent the person who assigns the job and why? Do we do it because the job has intrinsic meaning to us or is it a means of earning a living and nothing more? Is the work interesting or boring, is it congruent with our value system or at odds with it? What is the place of authority? Do we view authority figures as benign, caring or do we feel we are being imposed upon, being taken advantage of and misused? What's the background?

Are there other considerations to explain this? Possible roots and explanations for the phenomena we are describing may lie in (1) reactions to authority, (2) reactions to the inevitability of death, (3) problems with empathy, (4) task vs. ego orientation and other psychological issues.

Self-abnegation as a defense against ownership: the case of Lynn:

Lynn feels paralyzed and doomed to sadness and depression. Lynn knows she's doing this to herself, but what can be expected considering where she came from. Her mother was an addict and her father enabled mother's addiction. Everything appeared great on the surface, but periodically within the confines of the home, her mother went off the deep end. She became crazed, impossible to talk to or relate to, and she became cruel, mean and vicious. Her shifts in behavior were unpredictable and stood in sharp contrast to the smart efficient woman she was when sober. Her outbursts created chaos and confusion and Lynn knew she could not count on her. If she became complacent and trusted her mother, Lynn would only be hurt and disappointed, so she withdrew into her friends and her studies. However, early in life, Lynn was aware that her upbringing was not normal and that she felt different from other children and their families. She never got over it. She had to fight her whole life to do well in school and to hold a job. Lynn has been through three marriages that ended in divorce for which she held herself responsible because of her anger and her mistreatment of her ex-husbands. She felt she couldn't help herself and avoided close relationships. She kept blaming herself for the marital failures and for the fact that she did not make more of her life. Lynn graduated from a first rate university but felt that this was a fluke. She felt she was an imposter and though she was successful in her career, she believed that she could not aspire to anything better than what she had. The result is that she goes to work and stays home alone. She does not want to go out for fear that she will only alienate others.

Lynn is afraid to expose her self to others. She is certain that she will alienate them and then become hurt and angry. She detests herself and others. She is fearful of losing control and of being controlled by others. She is mistrustful and wary.

It sounds as if Lynn is accountable for her behavior, it sounds as though she knows herself. However, behind this front of seeing her difficulties as her doing, she insists that she cannot change because she was so severely damaged by her inconsistent, unpredictable and chaotic upbringing. "See what I grew up with! I'm damaged, my family was damaged and I will damage others." Essentially, Lynn is taking refuge by blaming her mother and by insulating herself from trying life out, by changing. She is disavowing responsibility for changing her self and her future.

She is also protecting her mother by failing to confront her anger towards her mother. As long as she can blame her unhappiness on her upbringing, she does not have to change. In addition, by remaining in her unhappy state and attributing it to her background, she feels protected from exposing herself to new and different, even positive experiences. The status quo is preserved.

Reactions to the inevitability of death:

When a job is done, it's over. Completion means the end. We allay our fears of death by keeping things open, unfinished, incomplete, still alive. When Steve was eight years old he would not take a bite out of an ice cream cone because if he did, he feared that there would be that much less left to eat. Eating meant using up and destroying and Steve loved ice cream and he wanted to preserve it. The motto was "don't finish anything, because that means the end."

Some of us resist growing up. We want to stay the child, to maintain the status quo. Growing up means growing old and dying so better remain immature. Find a place of blissful comfort and stay there, protect it from change and stop time. The goal is to avoid change, avoid using up anything. Spending money and spending time is using up the time and money forever. Time and money spent can never be recaptured. Yet time and money are two measures of reality – they are tangible, finite, measureable and irreplaceable. Once time is used up, it cannot be recouped. Once money is used up, there remains less than had it not been spent. So it's crucial to cheat reality by not spending time or money. The goal is not to maintain a dynamic living system, but to preserve forever a static and never-changing state. Protect from change, stop time, don't move, don't change, delay everything, avoid finality and death.

Steve's fear of change is understandable when placed in the context of his background. When he was three years old, his mother died of cancer. He was cared for by a well-meaning nanny who, however, could not replace his mother. Though he did not grasp the concept of death, he knew that the love and caring he had from his mother was taken away from him. He had to preserve whatever he had.

Problems with empathy:

Can we hear, tune in, identify with another person, while not necessarily agreeing with that other person? Can we put ourselves in the other person's shoes and sense how our behavior will impact them. Are we so focused on our selves that we are oblivious and insensitive to the affect we have upon others? Most of us sense whether our remarks or our actions will please or displease the other person, whether we will put them at ease or threaten them. When we find ourselves offending others without knowing that we are doing it, something is interfering with our ability to identify with the feelings of others. We overreact or under-react to the behavior of others. We over - personalize and distort remarks made by others but we are insensitive to our impact upon them. We know that we are hurt, but we fail to realize that we are hurting others.

Narcissism and self-centeredness numbs our sensitivity to others and we become immune to our impact on them. We view our behavior only in terms of ourselves.

We keep appointments that fulfill us, we dismiss commitments that do not fulfill us. We finish tasks that provide gratification and we leave tasks unfinished that do not provide fulfillment and gratification. Situations and people exist to please us. We do whatever is necessary to bring about a desired result. We may be exquisitely sensitive to those people and situations that can give us what we want and those that cannot. We manipulate and cajole to get what we want without being aware that we are doing it.

As a result, when we don't care, we are late for appointments or we delay finishing work. And when it's important to us, we are on time for appointments and we get work ready promptly. We deny any other motives because we are not aware that we are fulfilling our narcissistic needs.

For present purposes, we focus on the place of narcissism in delaying, avoiding, and being insensitive to the needs of others.

We all have an internal "radar system" that receives and sends messages. Those who lack empathy have radar systems that are not calibrated accurately. They misinterpret messages that were transmitted and they distort their messages to us.

For all their show of superiority to others, narcissistic individuals are troubled individuals who doubt themselves and suffer feelings of inferiority with needs to prove how competent, capable and charming they are. But if and when this narcissistic façade is punctured, the individual is devastated. His or her world comes to an end and the façade of grandiosity comes tumbling down.

A common echo of behavior from the past when there is an absence of empathy is exposure to caretakers who lack constancy and consistency. This results in an unconscious process of internal scanning and vigilance of others for evidence of being neglectful, ignoring and abandoning. This is a reaction to trauma of being separated from those who were expected to be present, constant and supportive. The trauma is of being abandoned and dismissed. As a result, there is an extreme vigilant expectation that no one can be relied upon. The wish for closeness is countered by mistrust and chronic feelings of vulnerability and defensive distancing. Hence, while intimacy and trust is craved, it is also dangerous. Such individuals tend to get close and then push away. They do to others what they expect and fear others will do to them. To allow closeness is to allow exposure to hurt. This becomes a repetitive and vicious cycle of closeness and alienation again and again.

Echoes of past voices are major contributors to narcissism and absence of empathy. Parents who are more concerned with themselves, their convenience and comforts at the expense of their children are a prime example. Fathers who are always too busy to be home, mothers who would rather raise "latchkey" kids who come home from school to an empty house while mother is playing bridge with friends are examples. When children feel ignored and neglected, despite the fact that they have a baby sitter at home, they sense that they are interfering with the interests and involvements of their parents. They feel they are in the way, that significant figures in their lives have little time for them. When parents are focused on themselves, children react by focusing on themselves. Children sense when parents are preoccupied with primping themselves, concerned with how they look and how they stand in the community. They know that they, the children, are either unimportant or are being used to aggrandize their parents.

Control: themes and variations

In our technological, achievement-oriented world, we are taught early in life to live up to demands and expectations of efficiency, perfectionism, speed, correctness, and neatness. We treat our spouses, our children and ourselves as if they should be well-oiled machines. We take for granted and without question that we should get more done, make more money, win more awards and trophies and accolades. We must be in control and through the exertion of control, we become outstanding and we demonstrate that we are in control of ourselves and of the world around us. And that is the most important thing. We must be in control; we must keep everything in control so that nothing gets out of hand.

We live in fear of our spontaneous urges and impulses, which must be suppressed, inhibited and controlled. We cannot accept the fact that we are living organisms. Rather, the goal is to become automatons.

We also live in fear of the world around us lest we be assaulted by man, nature or other forces.

Parents question their children at the end of the day and every day:

"Did you win the game?"

""Did you get the trophy?"

"Did you get A's?"

Rarely do parents ask:

"How do you feel?"

"Did you think of something new?"

"Have you had interesting thoughts?"

"How are your friends?"

Our focus is on accomplishment. We are compulsive, we must do, we must check, we dare not trust ourselves. We are preoccupied with details and goals and efficient ways to get to the goal.

We neglect critical and creative thinking. Instead we focus on learning and remembering in order to regurgitate information that, in turn, will result in better grades, promotions, and more money. We get rewarded for thinking inside the box and not outside the box. We are trained to do what is prescribed. We do not rely on ourselves and our own standards as the yardstick for success. Instead we allow ourselves to be defined by others, by our competition, by the company, by the boss.

This represents the ground that serves as the setting in which we, as individuals serve as the figure. Out surrounding world places a premium on regimentation, production, materialism and control often at the expense of other settings including dimensions such as family ties, relationships, thoughts and feelings. There is a conflict of values with many gradations. Not all people who pursue material ends do so at the cost of neglecting more enduring values and vice versa. However, in order to view the person against differing backgrounds, it helps to underline the contrasts.

Inner voices from the past are related to identifications with early relationships. We are taught and rewarded for abiding by and aping the behaviors of the adults in our lives. We become preoccupied with the standards of the group, to behave in ways that conform to the group even if we sacrifice our own standards and perceptions.

What makes some people followers and others leaders? Why do some of us conform while others rebel? Why are some of us dependent seeking the support of others while others are independent and strike out on their own? Why do some of us yield to group pressures while others stick to their own judgments even if it means going against the tide. There is much evidence supporting individual differences along these lines. There are those who obey authority even when they are commanded to commit inhuman and unethical acts while others refuse at the risk of punishment and ostracism.

Horace grew up in a home that was extremely religious, that demanded obedience to the commandments of the church, seeking the advice of the church leader at every turn to be certain that one would be free of sin. Parents, siblings, the community were all geared towards this belief-system that was deemed the only right and just way. Horace behaved like others in the community seeking approval and acceptance from those around him. But Horace reached a point in his development when he began to question the validity of the tenets of the religion and the group. Such questioning was frowned upon, but Horace could not dismiss his curiosity. At first he kept his thoughts to himself. He clandestinely read books that did not follow the prescribed beliefs and strictures. He thought, he questioned, he wondered. He could no longer contain himself and began to openly raise questions to his parents and the community. He could no longer follow the "straight and narrow." He was told to bury his sinful questions and to pray. He wanted to explore the wider outside world, to discover other ideas. He was brought before the elders of the community/congregation and was told that he would be ostracized from all the blessings and supports provided by the church. Horace had to break away though this meant paying a severe price of isolation and ostracism.

Why was it that Horace did this and not the hundreds or thousands of others who remained loyal to the church? His environment was essentially the same as the other members of that community, yet he was the maverick. He had no mentor who supported his separation, he had no outside encouragement to give him the strength and will to break from the established community, but he did. We do not have a clear answer as to why Horace did this while others did not. Most of us rest content finding security in belonging to the larger group and following expected behavior. We complain about the corporate environment and about having to abide by the structure of the job in terms of hours, vacation times allotted, salary, benefits, even covering over illegal activities etc., but when offered the option of striking out independently, taking the risks entailed in beginning new and different ventures, or joining the whistle blowers, many of us cannot take the risk. Most of us choose to take the more secure path rather than to try the unknown and the unpredictable.

What differentiates the "whistle blower," the person who refuses to go along with behavior, which may be unethical or even harmful to others, while others do as they are told, suspending their own values and beliefs. The person who refuses to go along with the injustices of Enron or the tortures at Abu Ghraib places his/her job at risk and is viewed as an outsider or even a traitor. Many of us are conditioned to look the other way, to avoid causing trouble. Others cannot abide these injustices and speak out. It is not merely a matter of ethical principles, but rather the ability to stand up to authority, to the pressures of the group, the demands for conformity, to maintain the boundaries that articulate the distinction between figure and ground while appreciating that all of us are influenced by out backgrounds and surroundings. To what degree do we allow ourselves to assert ourselves as figure against the ground and to what degree does the ground define our identity.

Yielding to the pressures of the group versus not- yielding is consistent. Studies demonstrate consistency across different venues in one's tendencies to yield or not to yield to group pressures, but as yet, there have been no identifiable personality characteristics that differentiate those who conform from those who do not. Such failure to identify personality traits was also seen in efforts to understand perpetrators of murder and atrocities by Nazi commandants in concentration camps who chose those who would be killed and those who would be sent to labor camps. They defended their actions on the grounds that they were following orders. They claimed that they had to yield to pressures of the group and pressures exerted by authority. There were those who refused to conform, often at the price of their lives. Man has the ability emotionally to detach himself, his intellect, his feelings and values and to conform to acts, which are at odds with basic values.

Why are some people prone to conform, to follow the pressures exerted by the group and by authority figures while others resist? Is yielding to such pressures related to conformity in general? Is not yielding related to rebellion? Can one resist such pressures without necessarily being rebellious? What are the roots that determine whether one submits to group pressures or does not submit? And what has this got to do with motivation for succeeding in achieving one's goals in life?

It is difficult to maintain beliefs and standards when others around us challenge them. But one might ask, "What about the all those who are non-conformists, who seem to be rebels?" Non-conformity does not represent independence. The rebel is still tied up with those he or she is rebelling against, the non-conformist is opposing conformity. The truly independent person has ideas which may or may not be in line with others, but they are his/her ideas and if they conform to the standards of others, that is fine and if they are not in line with the standards of others, that's fine too. Independence is not defiance. It is not being concerned about being part of the group or of winning praise. Rather it is a matter of trusting and pursuing one's convictions without coercion.

Gender Considerations

Most of us have grown up in a world of rapidly changing attitudes towards sex and gender. The result is that voices from the past have been changing, inconsistent and confusing. If it were simply a matter that relations between significant figures in our lives were clear and we, as younger people, were going through an "adolescent rebellion," that would be expected. But adults themselves have been going through their own revolution. Women are a significant part of the work force, they are better educated than ever before, they are opting to have fewer children and to have careers. They are not contented staying home and they are not idly accepting the so-called "glass ceiling" that limited their advancement and promotions in their careers. They are fighting this and are achieving higher positions than ever before and earning much more money.

By the same token, men are often earning less and holding lesser positions than their female counterparts. There are more "Mr. Moms" than ever before with men staying home to care for children while women work. Some men accept this, some feel diminished, and many are confused. These gender changes often fly in the face of voices from the past that dictated behavior that adheres to the norm, to the traditional, to identifying with parents. Stay-at-home mothers have difficulty when their adult married daughters opt to pursue a career.

Divorce is part of the histories of many people who are now parents. Divorce previously was the exception and somewhat shameful. It is now a significant factor in many people's backgrounds. In addition, "fused" families are frequent. Children of a marriage on the mother's side live with the children of the father's previous marriage with efforts to create a new family.

There are serial marriages exposing families to rapid and far-reaching changes.

In many instances now parents are not married, Couples are living together, single mothers abound without the stigma that had been rampant in such circumstances in the past. Gay marriages with children are becoming common and have legal status with financial responsibilities and obligations. Parenting by gay couples is more accepted.

Transexual choices are occurring with greater frequency.

But amidst all the change, some things remain constant. Power struggles, vying for domination and control continue whether people are married or living together, whether they have children, whether the woman or man is home rearing the child, whether the child's parents are a man and a woman, two women or two men, whether one parent is of a different racial or religious background than the other. To an increasing extent, in the realm of gender relations, echoes of the past do not reverberate or are not accepted often because the echoes are thin, lacking in substance and relevance.

The long-term fallout of all these changes is unknown. We know that previous standards are being up-ended. The traditional notion that children need a nuclear family consisting of a mother and father is being questioned. Yet we know that divorce exacts a heavy emotional toll on children and often, on spouses. Children wish and hope that their estranged or divorced or remarried parents would reunite. We also know that children of divorce, whether child, adolescent or adult, often react to parents' divorce with feelings of disillusionment. Parents lose credibility in the eyes of their children. Children react with feelings that their parents do not have their own act together and the result often is that the children feel that their parents owe them compensation for breaking up the family. Parents become check writers and banks to many children of divorce. We do not know what the future of marriage and child-rearing will be. There are no templates and fewer echoes of voices from the past.

In all of the above - cited scenarios we would do well to consider the "echoes of voices from the past" as examples of relational determination. If we understand behavior within the framework of the surrounding field consisting of a person's background in all of its manifestations including attitudes that have been internalized from family, friends, culture, religion, etc., the behavior which may, at first seem strange and bizarre becomes more comprehensible and seems to make sense.

Addictions and Control

In a book about control, it is crucial to consider those who feel unable to gain control of their lives. Consider alcohol and drug addiction, consider addiction to sugar and addiction to gambling. These addictions destroy lives and families because of feelings of helpless in the face of unrelenting needs to ingest substances resulting in a loss of control over one's life. The substance abuser feels helpless in his/her need for alcohol, drugs or sugar. There is a wish to be in control that conflicts with a striving to be free of control. The genetic/biological issues involved are real and significant complicating factors.

Addicts may try desperately to control their cravings, but to little avail. Though many would not admit it, they feel like failures. The alcoholic promises that he will stop drinking, the obese sugar-addicted person promises the family or the physician that they will lose weight, but the promises are broken.

Lives are lived in states of anxiety and anticipation. Will she be drunk when I come home? Will he be spaced out? Did he go to his job today? Will she be gorging on bonbons? Sometimes the anticipation and the anxiety is well - founded and sometimes it is not. One can never be sure. The housewife can be a meticulous homemaker making certain that everything is in place only to resort to drinking and becoming irritable and slovenly. The overeater may try every diet out there and may lose 50 or 75 pounds, only to gain the weight back to the disappointment of everyone including him/herself.

The addictions are rooted in genetics and in biological predispositions, but they area also responses to voices from the past. The genetic and biological contributions are significant and potent. The possibility of ethnic/genetic pre-=dispositions cannot be dismissed. Sensitivity, especially to alcohol, is seen in certain ethnic groups in far greater numbers than in others. This may also be the case for addiction to drugs, sugar, etc. However, not all children of addicts become addicts. It is necessary to consider an intersection of the biological with the environmental. There are those relatively rare individuals who are able to stop on their own. "cold turkey" so to speak. Some people feel that they have reached bottom and are able to stop gratifying the addiction. Some addicts are confronted by family and friends who lovingly express concern and worry and succeed in reaching them so that they stop. But for most addicted individuals, The Twelve-Step[1] program succeeds the best, often following a period of rehabilitation. Individual psychotherapy is useful following termination of the active addiction, but it is rarely effective while a person is using alcohol or drugs or binge eating.

Despite the fact that the addict may express feelings of remorse and feelings of having failed themselves and others and despite behavior, which is clearly not under his control, the addict lives under the illusion that he/she is in control to the point of being grandiose. Though he may be beset with fear, the addict eradicates fears by imbibing in alcohol, drugs, and sugars. The alcoholic does not want to be told that he is in no condition to drive, because as far as he is concerned, he is perfectly capable of driving. The obese sugar addict does not want to be told to diet because she insists that she does not overeat. But she also feels powerful with her 350 pounds. If she loses weight, she panics because she feels weaker and more vulnerable. The alcoholic is king of the mountain under the influence, but when not drinking, he is just another person and that is not acceptable. There is tremendous resistance to relinquishing the illusion of grandiosity and the fantasy that "I am the master of my fate; I am the captain of my soul."

The voices from the past echo as well. For example, "I drink so it's OK if you drink. I can be in control and so can you. I overeat and it's OK if you overeat. Let others accept us as we are and not as they want us to be."

Why is The Twelve Step program helpful? Why is the Serenity Prayer [2] the touchstone of alcoholics anonymous? If we can understand the roots of the effectiveness of these contributions, we may be in a better position to understand the addictions.

The Serenity Prayer and the Twelve Step program serve as antidotes to the illusion of grandiosity. They have in common the belief that one needs help, that one cannot relinquish the addiction by himself or herself or with the help of another human being. The illusion of grandiosity of the addict requires the intervention of superhuman power which represents both a recognition and an acceptance of one's limitations, but also a recognition that one's addiction is so strong that it cannot be controlled by mere human effort and will.

Grandiosity is crucial to understanding the need to control. The underlying dynamic is that if things get out of control, cataclysmic events can be released. It is therefore essential that I keep myself in control because terrible things can happen.

Implicit in the Twelve Step Program and in The Serenity Prayer, is an acceptance of dependency. The addict's illusory need to believe that he is invulnerable, totally independent, and totally in control is tempered, muted, and modified. The message is that dependency, error and vulnerability are OK so long as a supreme power is in control.

Grandiosity is relieved and one is permitted to admit shortcomings and weaknesses.

What are the echoes from the past in the addictions?

In the case of those who are addicted and are children of addicts, the message may be to be like me, enable the perpetuation of the addiction and the rationalizations of the addiction. It may be conformity to the voices of the past.

Footnotes

¹The Twelve Step program

1. Admit powerlessness over alcohol-that my life has become unmanageable
2. A higher power can restore me to sanity
3. Decide to turn our will over to God as we understand him
4. Make a searching and fearless moral inventory of ourselves
5. Admit to God, ourselves, and to another human being the exact nature of our wrongs
6. Stand ready to have God remove all these defects of character
7. Ask Him to remove our shortcomings
8. Make a list of all persons we harmed and be willing to make amends to all of them
9. Make direct amends to such people provided it would not injure them or others
10. Continue to take personal inventory and when we were wrong, to promptly admit it
11. Seek through prayer and meditation to improve our conscious contact with God as we understand him
12. Try to carry this message to alcoholics and practice these principles in all our affairs

footnote

[2] The Serenity Prayer
God grant me the serenity
 to accept the things I cannot change;
 courage to change the things I can;
 and wisdom to know the difference.

Living one day at a time;
Enjoying one moment at a time;
Accepting hardships as the pathway to peace
Taking, as He did, this sinful world
as it is. Not as I would have it
Trusting that He will make all things right
If I surrender to His Will
That I may be reasonably happy in this life
and supremely happy with Him
Forever in the next
Reinhold Niebuhr

6

CHANGING THE ECHOES OF INNER VOICES

THE FEELINGS OF inferiority, inadequacy and helplessness that haunt so many people regardless of how objectively successful they are, lead to tendencies to compensate, to prove how strong and competent they are. The echoes of voices from the past of criticism by parents, mockery by other children, of never feeling good enough, strong enough, smart enough, of not living up to the expectations of parents and teachers keep sounding and resounding. Repeated attempts to deny, overcome and compensate for the damage to self- esteem do not relieve the problem. Objective success does not quiet these voices because we are obsessed with those who are more successful, smarter, more accomplished than we are. So we erect grandiose expectations. We have to be the best at whatever we do and anything less will not satisfy us. We need to be in control of ourselves and the world and those around us. We tend to be rigid and inflexible fearing that if we bend, terrible things would happen. The common response to such feelings is to raise one's level of aspiration, to go after what one wants, to be impatient and intolerant of those who accept less than the greatest. The middle -aged man strives to prove how young, successful, strong and vital he is. He needs to be top dog, to ride around in his sports car, to carouse with women other than his wife, to drink too much, and to boast of his accomplishments.

It is not only our own needs to succeed, but our society places a premium on aiming for the top, to be superior, to beat the competition.

It is only when we can accept ourselves and feel that we are good enough that we no longer have to run on a treadmill of constantly proving ourselves. It is not a matter of feeling complacent, but rather of accepting ourselves as human beings with our assets and liabilities so that we can ease up on our needs to be controlled and to control others.

We have seen that many of us are dominated by echoes of voices from the past often filling us with anxiety and with needs to live up to the expectations and the demands of others. We lose our sense of identity in the service of trying to be who we are not. We do not know whether our actions are being motivated by ourselves or whether we are reacting to voices from the past that insisted that theirs was the only right way and that all other ways were wrong. We don't have freedom of choice.

Many of us find comfort and solace in abiding by and adhering to the echoes of past voices and we do not experience this as control. We are happy to perpetuate the past and to conform to the standards that we were taught and to model ourselves after our parents and mentors. We do not experience conflict. We feel at ease doing things and thinking things that are the same as or similar to those who raised us. The identification is free of conflict and congruent with the image we have of ourselves. Within the context of positive feelings that are free of conflict, we feel at home carrying on traditions and rituals that we grew up with. We do not have to fight this because we do not feel controlled. We are at one with our history and ourselves But many of us need to spread our own wings and feel that we are free of past voices, past encumbrances.

There are many of us who cannot feel comfortable with those echoes from the past that keep resounding. We need to express our own ideas, to try new and different styles, to assert our individuality and autonomy. We may have felt dominated and controlled by parents and we may feel that now, as adults, we want to be free. Some of us seek freedom by controlling and dominating others, Some of us simply want to do things our way. Some of us view our past environments as alien and unacceptable. We strive for a different life style and we renounce the past.

Victor expressed such a scenario. He recalled that as a child from the ages seven through eleven his mother would dress him up in a suit and tie and take him on Saturday afternoons to concerts or operas. He went because he had no choice. As he approached eleven years of age he insisted that he did not want to go on anymore of these outings. His mother was hurt, but he told her he really hated the concerts and wanted to spend time with his friends. Victor began listening to hard rock music on the radio and on his CDs much to the chagrin of this mother. If he heard classical music or opera, he would turn it off. Victor became quite knowledgeable about rock music and played keyboard with his friends who played amplified rock instruments. Victor eventually went on to college studying while listening to hard rock playing in the background. He went to many rock concerts. He would avoid classical music at college at all costs. Victor turned thirty. He was driving his car to work one day and happened to hear some classical music on the radio. He recognized the music from the concerts he attended when he was much younger and thought to himself that this music was pretty good. He did not change the station. If fact, he began to enjoy listening to classical music and even opera when he wanted to. He was not cajoled into it. He was able to enjoy it. The echoes of inner voices from the past that he abhorred now became desirable.

Lenny grew up in an Orthodox Jewish home, one in which most of the laws and rituals were observed. This was integral to the family's culture. Lenny went away to college and, though he was signed up for Kosher meals and participated in the college's Hillel, he questioned the practices that he grew up with. He studied other cultures, other religions, and alternate ways of life. He became skeptical of many of the practices that he had accepted. Lenny decided no longer to adhere so closely to the echoes of inner voices from his past. He became less observant, he ate foods that were not Kosher, at first with great anxiety, but he eventually felt his behavior to be quite natural. Several years after college, Lenny went to Rome on business and his hotel was close to the Synagogue. Though he had not attended services for many years, on Saturday morning, he saw people going to the Synagogue. He thought it would be interesting to attend services in a foreign country. Lenny felt tremendous pangs of nostalgia during the services and he felt quite transformed. When he returned home, he became much more active in his local Synagogue, but in a more liberal and flexible manner than had been the case when he was a child. His return was on his on terms and in his own way. He felt good about that.

When we grow up in an environment that is unpredictable, inconstant, and destructive, we feel damaged ourselves. These early feelings of insecurity can be repaired if we have opportunities to express our anger, disappointment and feelings of failure. It is baggage that burdens us and prevents us from feeling free to express our individuality. Without the chance to express such feelings, we are left with baggage that is transformed into a variety of unconscious defenses and character defects that impact our entire life.

The solution is not, as it too often is, to repeat the past, to dominate, control and undermine others. Instead, it is freeing our selves from the echoes of past voices and finding our own voice. We all have to write our own story in a way that is unique to us, a story that only could be written by one author. Not necessarily the best story nor the most remarkable story, but a story that is authentic, owned and cherished. Not a story blaming others, or to seeking revenge, but the heartfelt story that only I could write.

Creating such a narrative is what psychotherapy is about. Cutting through the grandiosity, the angers, feelings of failure, freeing one's self from defensiveness, camouflage and subterfuge. It means accepting and avowing that this is who I am, these are my choices based upon my self-awareness. This is necessary to be able determine and to define a sense of authentic identity.

This sense of identity is aided by owning and accepting one's "time line." The time line refers to the totality of one's history extending from birth to the present time. This includes a recognition of the up's and down's in one's life, the gaps, the smudges in one's history. The tendency is to repress, suppress, deny and avoid the down's, the mistakes, the regrets, the shameful failures that are part of the time line. However, a cohesive sense of self, an integrated sense of identity means owning the negative with the positive. The hurts, the traumas, the failures, as well as the successes, the rewards and awards all of which constitute one's self. A goal of psychoanalytic psychotherapy is to help make what is unconscious, conscious. This means allowing the emergence of the secrets, the memories, the shame and the guilt - producing experiences in one's history and owning them. No longer burying them, but giving them fresh air for examination, for understanding and for owning them as part of one's life.

The fact is that there is a heavy price to pay for detaching portions of one's life's experiences because what is repressed distorts one's view of one's own self and life and comes to haunt you in the future. Such inhibition of portions of one's history leads to inauthenticity, to becoming an imposter with an inner sense of being phony.

Insight is a first step in establishing a sense of autonomy, an ability to assume accountability for one's actions and choices. But knowing is not enough. Growing up is growing away from, a readiness to decide which echoes of voices from the past we wish to maintain and which we wish to be free of. To do this requires sufficient awareness and objectivity to enable us to evaluate where we came from, who we are and who we strive to be. It means allowing ourselves to mourn the passing of earlier beliefs and attachments, finding new environments that are more congruent with our perceptions and judgments. It means freeing ourselves from guilt for daring to be different and doing things differently. The goal is not rebellion, but rather autonomy, the ability to choose not to be controlled and not to control others. Relinquishing earlier and persistent attachments, protections, loyalties, and fears is extremely difficult. For many, it is a life-long struggle that exacts a heavy toll. Others have shucked off attachments and are not bound by loyalties, but the price for this emotional detachment is heavy.

To a large extent, what we know, our insights, and our intellectual grasp of our situation is, for many, a sacred cow. We believe that the path to emotional change is through insight. This is false. We all know people who have been through years of psychotherapy, who have an intellectual grasp of their problems and are able to talk about them with insight and understanding, but who have not changed. They continue repeating the same patterns of behavior again and again. Insight is an important beginning to the process of change, but it is not enough unless there is a process of digestion, absorption and internalization. This often requires a period of mourning, of emotionally separating and distancing one's self from those who have been closest and most influential in our lives. We realize that such attachments, as comforting and supportive as they were, may have also prevented us from developing ourselves as mature and separate human beings. The separation can be extremely painful, but if the relationship is based upon a more solid footing than one of infantile dependency, the relationship can be restored, albeit on a different and more mature level.

Giving up the echoes of voices from the past means retaining what we feel is worthwhile and what is congruent with our personalities and being able to free our selves from the echoes of past voices which are not congruent with the kinds of life we want to live without guilt and misgivings. It means opening the door for change so that we no longer have to be vigilant about who is being controlled and who is controlling. A goal of psychodynamic psychotherapy is having freedom to choose between alternatives and to make choices based upon a full recognition of alternatives. It means a willingness to make choices with a sense of full accountability the choice is made with full awareness and responsibility whether or not it turns out well. Being able to appreciate that living in a state of fear or of needing to prove that one is in control is based upon feeling inadequate and is ultimately self-sabotaging. It means distinguishing emotionally and intellectually the delusion of being in control vs. the reality of being in control.

The resolution, the freedom from the echoes from the past also means relinquishing the conviction that the echoes are holy, that they have been handed down by superior beings and that we must aspire to be superior, even grandiose beings. It is necessary to let go of the belief that we are or that we are destined to be superior to others and that we must be beyond criticism and beyond reproach.

Related to this is a shift in the way we view life from seeking status and position to seeing life as an ongoing process. The pursuit of position, status or tangible accomplishment deprives us of an appreciation of ourselves as human beings who can change with circumstances and with the world around us.

Accepting the fact that our surrounding world and our ways of perceiving that world are often built-in and have to be accepted no matter where we are. They are part of being human. The perception of moving when you are stationary as a train passes is not something we can dismiss or change just as the color of a red disc surrounded by blue is seen differently than the same red disc when it is surrounded by green.

This ability to change what is changeable and to accept what is part of our world is a tall order, which some people seem able to arrive at by themselves. For most of us, it is not so easy and psychotherapy based upon self-discovery and self-examination is the avenue of choice. This unearthing process is to be differentiated from modifying behavior. The change we refer to is personality change that comes from a restructuring and shifting of the ways in which we see ourselves and our world. In many instances, it requires a shift from viewing ourselves as immortal powerhouses to mortal human beings with foibles, struggles and with needs to compromise. Such change stands in contrast to a process that relies primarily on behavioral or intellectual change

7

THE LARGER CANVAS

OUR FOCUS TO this point has been about control issues in our individual lives and in our immediate surroundings.

We try to keep things in order and most of us abhor chaos. Lest we lose control over ourselves and our environment, we try to impose order and control over others. We have seen how parents do this to children, how bosses do it to employees, how siblings and co-workers do this to each other, how spouses do this to each other. Control is imposed in a variety of ways; through power or weakness, through boldness or manipulation, through begging or through emotional blackmail, etc. Generally, we dislike chaos, though we often bring chaos with us due to fears that we will not be able to cope as well as we think we ought to and we often become overwhelmed with anxiety. We bring these concerns with us in our inner lives, in our immediate family relations, and in our work and social relationships.

Is there a relationship between voices from the past on an individual level to the world on a broader scale. If, as individuals, we are stuck in cycles of repetition, can we also say that history on larger scale repeats itself? Do we learn from our mistakes? It's been said that progress is built upon the shoulders of preceding geniuses, but can we also say that we keep reinventing the wheel, and that the definition of experience is making the same mistakes again and again? Santayana has written:

"Those who cannot remember the past are condemned to repeat it." However, there are many instances in which we remember the past and repeat it anyway.

And what about decisions we make and actions we take based upon the information or misinformation we receive? We were told that there was intelligence data indicating that Iraq had weapons of mass destruction and many in high places voted to wage war in Iraq only to learn that the so-called intelligence was wrong. We depend on what we know and what we perceive to form our judgments and decisions. What happens when that is turned upside down?

Can we make the leap from the individual to the larger group and to the world around us? A person stands on a railroad platform pretty sure of who he is in his surroundings. A train rolls by and the person is confused. He knows that he is standing on a stationary platform, but now he is not so sure. The train passes and he is confused. Is he moving? Is the train moving? The surroundings shift and he no longer has the confidence that he is stationary and standing in one place. Does the group do this to the individual? If our judgment is challenged by a group. do we yield our perception to the pressure of a group or do we resist it insisting that our perception, our judgment is correct. Are we dominated by our environment or do we try to assert individual choices which may be at odds with that environment. Arab nations lived for many years under dictatorships and there was relative calm and order. The Arab Spring arose overthrowing vested powers and chaos resulted. Are we either puppets in the hands of powerful dictators or are we herds of wild people? Are we influenced in our perceptions, our judgments, our thinking or by environmental forces some of which we are not aware of? Do we have autonomy or is this an illusion?

We seek power to affirm our beliefs and we often attempt to impose our beliefs on others. Spouses assert power over each other and parents do the same with children and so do bosses over employees, etc. On the social scale, we try to influence others, to impress them, to compete with them. We, in turn, are influenced by others in our surroundings. Is this competitiveness for the good of others or to assert our superior strength? Legislators supposedly represent the best interests of their constituents. Yet we know that power corrupts. Legislators are influenced by power - grabbers and lobbyists, by their own greed and by their own prejudices and the public be damned. Countries are influenced by power-hungry dictators and by richer countries that promise favors or by governments that rattle sabers, etc.

In history, the nobility has suppressed the proletariat causing major revolutions. There are those who seek to gain and preserve status and to maintain the status quo. They view life and themselves as well as their world in terms of prestige and position. They want to preserve vested power. They do not view life as an ongoing fluid and ever-changing process.

Individuals seek to achieve goals, to gain status in order to bolster themselves and to feel that they have arrived. They attempt to gratify their narcissistic needs so they can feel superior to others. This is short-lived when they discover that others surpass them.

Nations seek to be dominant and to suppress smaller and poorer nations so they can gain power over people and land giving them the illusion that they wield power. It is not long before they find themselves in the midst of upheavals with new boundaries.

Individuals change, families change, nations and boundaries change. Climate changes causing significant changes in the productivity and viability of certain geographical areas. To what degree do we fight such changes in order to maintain things the way they have been? When do we confront changes that occur and when do we recognize that such changes are inevitable and beyond our control. When do we plan for change as part of our plan for the future? It is difficult to accept that we cannot stop time and change, but such recognition and planning is crucial. It requires a shift from a view of life as a static state to changing process. The Greek philosopher, Heraclitus, observed that we don't step into the same stream twice. A stream is ever-changing and so is life. However, there are many ways in which the stream remains the same such as location, geography, etc. Voices from the past echo: "Never again" "The war to end all wars," Yet genocide continues despite the museums and memorials that testify to such horrors. Countries continue to war against internal rebellions as well as against other nations. Unfortunately, "the more things change, the more they stay the same."

We resist accepting climate warming and increasing unpredictable weather, so we rebuild after a storm without recognizing that other storms will follow with as much or more devastation.

On Narcissism, Arrogance and Self-Sabotage:

Individuals fight against odds in attempts to save face, to feel they have significance, and, in some instances, to prove their superiority and their immortality. Some are short (Napoleon), some are poor, some feel defeated (Hitler), some feel inferior. Some seek compensatory power and succeed followed by actions that undermine their success. Some feel invincible and they gamble with the expectation that their success will continue unabated since they are above the usual limitations, beyond scrutiny and criticism. They believe that succeeding is a given. World leaders gain fame and power only to push limits to the point of defeat. Individuals do the same. Individuals and political leaders seem to repeat risks again and again to prove invincibility and mastery over all possibilities? Is there a need in man to replace success with failure, to repeat the cycle that life must be followed by death, that anabolic processes must be followed by catabolic processes? Can this cycle be explained in terms of guilt and feelings of undeserving or are more potent factors operating? Is there an addiction to narcissism, to the euphoric feeling of being above others, a sense that death can be denied and defied and the usual restrictions on mortals do not apply in my case? Not only am I, the leader who is above limitations and restrictions, but I lead my community, my nation to a state of superiority? Is there a need to prove that no force will impose restrictions on me, including the force of mortality? Individuals sabotage themselves by trying to prove that they are not subject to limitations only to lose all that they have gained. World leaders do the same, convincing their constituents that they can rise up and defeat other forces.

Grandiose individuals who can brook no limitations often go down in defeat paying a terribly high price for their actions in order to prove that they can rise above limits of the common man. They refuse to accept restrictions or boundaries. There is little room for compromise. They genuinely believe that they can get away with gratifying themselves even if it hurts others or defies standards that they promised to uphold. They need to believe that they are superior, smarter, more cunning than most people only to find themselves defeated.

Similarly, political leaders, whether they are elected to office or achieve office through force, often get carried away with their power and believe that they can do whatever they wish without limitation only to be overpowered and even removed from office.

It is important for ordinary mortals as well as for world figures to own their humanity and their history. We all live in a social context, whether it is with our families, with friends, with community, or with national or international figures as followers or as leaders. We may be leaders, but history reminds us that it all is only for the time being.

ADDENDUM:

This addendum comes following the Newtown, Connecticut shooting of 20 children and six teachers at the Sandy Hook Elementary School. This tragedy follows several other mass killings in Colorado, Arizona, West Virginia, California and other states within the past few years. Such rampages do not occur on this scale or with such frequency in other countries. To understand this phenomenon, we must consider historical, cultural and psychological issues that contribute to the problem.

Historically, the United States Constitution contains the second amendment to the Bill of Rights that provides for "the right to bear arms." This provision was inserted to provide citizens the ability to protect themselves from hostile governments and other threats in a new and unsettled country. The Second Amendment has been used by the gun lobby to justify the possession of high powered automatic assault weapons without careful screening and supervision in a country that has become far more structured, densely populated and organized than it was many years ago. The colonies consisted of a new land that was viewed as uncivilized and populated by Indians who were considered savages. The settlers not only had to fight for independence from England, but they had to settle a vast land populated by those who had been on this land long before they arrived and did not want their land overtaken by aliens. A frontier culture was established that involved dividing the people between the "good" guys and "bad" guys, between cowboys and Indians. As the land settled, slaves were imported, bought and sold as chattel. A culture of segregation became part of the settling with masters and slaves dividing the country. The Civil War was fought between brothers at close range. It was a bloody war with Americans killing Americans. During the nineteenth and early twentieth centuries, there were mob lynchings, the KKK and intense segregation between whites and black.

In the early part of the twentieth century, prohibition was enacted which brought with it bootlegging and mob killings. We had cops and robbers. The result was a continuing belief that people had a reason and right to bear arms.

However, at the present time, we pride ourselves on having a more civilized society without the divisions cited above. But there are people who feel weak and impotent, who seek to compensate for their inadequacies and there are those who are emotionally disturbed who seek to ventilate their frustrations, live out delusional distortions and assert their power by controlling and dominating those who inhabit what are ordinarily peaceful and trusting environments. In our society we continue to revere those who appear to be strong, tough and powerful, the winners, those who pursue and get what they want. Among those who feel weak, inadequate and those who view themselves and are viewed by others as outsiders and misfits, there are is a tendency to turn energies inwardly and to create and live out fantasies that are not tested against reality. Some of these individuals live out hallucinatory wish-fulfilling thoughts and delusional distortions of being powerful, of gaining revenge, of gaining notoriety. When the defense mechanisms of such individuals are not intact either because of disordered thinking or because of the influence of drugs or alcohol, then the tendency is to turn fantasy into activity often with dire consequences. We also tend to equate fantasy with action. We believe that "evil thoughts are the same as evil acts" and hence, there is no reason not to act out evil if we have evil thoughts.

Such individuals also feel that they have little control over their own lives and attempt to compensate for their lack of control by asserting control over those who cannot defend themselves, e.g., children, innocent audiences, etc.

All countries in the world have some population of misfits. They do not have mass killings as we do in the United States. The combination of the frontier culture, the divisions within the society, and the easy access to killing weapons all contribute to the problem we have presently in the United States of America.

BIBLIOGRAPHY

Asch, S. (1952). *Social Psychology*. New York: Prentice-Hall

Asch, S. (1956). Studies on independence and conformity, Psychological Monographs, 70. 9 Whole no. 416)

Freud, S. (1958). *The Standard Edition of the Complete Works of Sigmund Freud*, 24 vols., translated by J. Strachey. London: Hogarth Press

Luepnitz, D.A, (2002), *Schopenhauer's Porcupines*. New York: Basic Books

Milgrim, S. (1974). Obedience to Authority, An Experimental View, Harper Collins.

Rosner, S. (1957). Consistency in response to group pressures. *The Journal of Abnormal and Social Psychology*, 35, 1, 145-146, July.

Rosner, S. and Hobe, L. (1974). *The Marriage Gap*. New York: David McKay.

Rosner, S. and Hermes, P. (2006). *The Self-Sabotage Cycle*. Westport, CT, Praeger.

Santayana, G. (1905). *The Life of Reason*, Vol.1, UK: Echo Library

Shabad, P. (1993). "Repetition and incomplete mourning. The intergenerational transmission of traumatic themes. *Psychoanalytic Psychology,* 10(1): 61-75.

Witkin, H.A. (et al). *Personality Through Perception: An Experimental and Clinical Study.* New York: Harper & Brothers.

Zimbardo , P. ((2007). The Lucifer Effect. *Understanding How Good* People *Turn Evil.* New York: Random House.

Stanley Rosner, Ph. D. is a clinical psychologist who has been in practice for 50 years. He is a Fellow of the American Psychological Association, Society for Personality Assessment and the Connecticut Psychological Association. He is a Diplomate in Clinical Psychology and in Psychoanalysis, American Board of Examiners in Professional Psychology He has served as President of the Connecticut Psychological Association and President of the Connecticut Society of Psychoanalytic Psychologists.

www.ingramcontent.com/pod-product-compliance
Lightning Source LLC
Chambersburg PA
CBHW070931290526
45795CB00001B/486